THE
UNPLUGGED
WOODSHOP

The Taunton Press

THE
UNPLUGGED
WOODSHOP

HAND-CRAFTED
PROJECTS FOR
THE
HOME & WORKSHOP

BY TOM FIDGEN

The Taunton Press

To Darrell, artist, inventor, prospector,
and friend. I wish you'd stayed around
to see this one through brother.
Rest in peace.
Darrell Darnell, 1967–2011

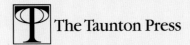
The Taunton Press

The Taunton Press, Inc., 63 South Main Street, PO Box 5506, Newtown, CT 06470-5506
e-mail: tp@taunton.com

Editor: Peter Chapman
Copy editor: Candace B. Levy
Indexer: Jay Kreider
Jacket/Cover design: Stacy Wakefield Forte
Interior design: Stacy Wakefield Forte
Layout: Stacy Wakefield Forte
Illustrator: Melanie Powell
Photographer: Tom Fidgen

The following names/manufacturers appearing in *The Unplugged Woodshop* are trademarks:
Bad Axe Tool Works™, Brusso®, Dumpster®, Forstner®, Irwin®, Lee Valley Tools®, Lie-Nielson®,
SketchUp®, Stanley®, Tried & True™, Veritas®, Woodcraft®

Library of Congress Cataloging-in-Publication Data

Fidgen, Tom.
 The unplugged workshop / Tom Fidgen.
    pages cm
 Includes index.
 ISBN 978-1-60085-763-8
 1. Woodwork. I. Title.
 TT180.F53 2013
 684'.08--dc23

Printed in the United States of America
10 9 8 7 6 5 4 3 2 1

ACKNOWLEDGMENTS

FOR CAROLYN, my beautiful partner through life, and our two amazing children, Piper and Nelson. Without the three of you by my side, this would not have been possible.

For Peter, my editor, the other side of these pages and one of the unsung heroes of the book.

For Robin, who at the eleventh hour on my path to self-publishing suggested I contact The Taunton Press. Good call!

For Anatole, for the warm welcome and introductions.

For Mark, a master saw maker. Thanks for the sawblades and the friendship.

For Josh, the best designer a guy could be related to! Many thanks for the logo.

For Sandy, my Web developer, my friend, and oftentimes my psychiatrist.

For everyone else through the rest of this book-making process: the artwork, production, printing, packaging, marketing, publicizing . . . basically, all of the work that happens after I write this! Without all of you, books never happen. Many thanks!

For you the reader, either here or online, it's for you these pages are made.

The Unplugged Woodshop started as a simple blog to share my thoughts and ideas about hand tools and furniture making. It has evolved organically into a friendly, global community that I feel privileged to be part of. A quiet revolution, when working together, a million hands crafting, this is when positive changes occur. Enjoy the time you spend working wood no matter what tools you use to work it with, every detail and every step of the way. Work makes life sweet.   www.theunpluggedwoodshop.com

 The Unplugged Woodshop is proud to be in partnership with 1% for the Planet. Members of 1% for the Planet contribute 1% of annual sales directly to nonprofit environmental organizations. The 1% for the Planet network brings together like-minded leaders who share a belief that business can be a vital catalyst for positive environmental change.

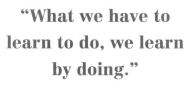

"What we have to learn to do, we learn by doing."

—Aristotle

CONTENTS

THE ART IN CRAFT

WELCOME TO the Unplugged Woodshop, where things are made by hand.

The pages of this book represent a year inside my woodshop, my unplugged woodshop, where I use only hand tools to craft objects from wood. So, why unplugged? Without sounding too clichéd, for me the journey is truly the destination. I enjoy the process of designing and building furniture by hand, from the initial sketches in my notebooks to visiting local mills and backyard woodcutters. I enjoy bringing home rough-cut planks of local hardwood and having them acclimatize to my shop space. I delight in discovering their grain patterns and the unique characteristics present in every piece of wood. Yes, even the arduous and physical demands of ripping, crosscutting, and resawing timber after the furniture parts have been carefully laid out are things I truly enjoy. Dimensioning the roughsawn lumber until the boards glisten under a handplaned surface. Laying out and executing fine joinery until the pieces come to life and final finishes are applied. Each step is as important and rewarding as the next.

From my small, 12-ft. by 12-ft. basement space in downtown Toronto, you'll be witness to a real-life documentation of handcraft in modern times. From the initial spark when inspiration ignites to the final finishes, hand-rubbed and ready to be delivered, the book will demonstrate what it means to work in and, perhaps more important, to imagine and create in a custom woodshop.

On some occasions that may mean building your own hand tools, and on other days we may be inventing new ones. The fact that I don't have a need to use any power tools in my work may inspire some woodworkers, but it is my hope that the designs will appeal to both the power-tool wood-workers, the blended woodshops, and those who have chosen to go unplugged as I have.

I'm proud and excited to offer my own unique style and voice to the trade of woodcraft. I'll challenge traditional ideas while I write about new ones. This is not a history book, but it is indeed a book of history. The projects I've chosen are inspired by my past. The forms have been reclaimed and recycled. It's my hope that this body of work has an aesthetic continuity that flows through all of the pieces while maintaining an individual style and panache. No two projects are ever really the same when the hand of the maker is present.

With techniques ranging from lamination to inlay, curved work, and mixing media, the technical side of the book will challenge the amateur to intermediate woodworker and, I hope, inspire the seasoned. Saw shopmade veneers, but only after you've made your own custom hand tools to do so, designed specifically for the required task. Use benchtop fixtures and jigs within dedicated work stations. We'll harness the inspiration and allow the mind's eye the time it needs to develop the design. With a pencil in hand and a promise to the heart that it makes "perfectly good sense" to use a handsaw instead of a bandsaw.

Take a few minutes each day and sketch your design ideas. Try to capture the moment, and, if you're really lucky, a small fraction of those ideas may come to fruition. Have a go and try making them one day— whatever they may happen to be. Life is a story, and we're all writing our own chapters. What will you decide to say?

Place rough stock cupped-side down on the bench to begin.

DIMENSIONING ROUGH LUMBER

DIMENSIONING ROUGH stock into square, smooth furniture parts is probably one of the most enjoyable steps in furniture making. With a freshly sharpened handplane, there really isn't a better way to get to know the wood you're using. For the benefit of anyone who isn't familiar with the process of dimensioning rough lumber by hand, here is a quick overview: Reference face to reference edge; reference edge to second edge and then opposite face for final thickness; crosscut ends for finished length. Let's take a closer look.

STEP 1: ESTABLISH A REFERENCE FACE

Begin by choosing a surface, or *face*. Base this decision on whatever surface is the flattest and place this flat surface face down on the benchtop. If the board is cupped, put the cupped side down for stability. Use wedges, if necessary, to hold the piece steady while you establish the first reference face.

I usually begin by taking a coarse shaving with a jack plane, working across the grain. If the stock is already reasonably flat and there isn't too much material to remove, I'll start with a jointing plane along the grain.

Plane the top surface of the plank until you have a smooth, flat face and

1. Winding sticks exaggerate any twist or wind in the stock. Here, the workpiece winds from the far left to the nearest right corner. 2. Plane diagonally between these areas and then the full face again until you see a flat face.

Check that the edge is square to the reference face.

check for wind using a set of winding sticks placed at each end of the workpiece. When you bend down and look across the sticks, you'll see an exaggerated view of any twist or wind in the workpiece. If any wind is detected, plane the high areas until the winding sticks show the workpiece is as flat as your handplane can make it. Label this first, flat surface the *reference face*; it is used to reference the rest of the dimensioning process.

STEP 2: ESTABLISH A REFERENCE EDGE

With the reference face flat and smooth, move to an edge. Use the first face to reference the edge and square the two surfaces together. If the edge is rough, use a jack plane to begin and follow with a jointer. Label this edge as the *reference edge*. These two surfaces will be used not only to reference the other two surfaces in this dimensioning process but also as reference for joinery layout throughout the rest of the project.

STEP 3: ESTABLISH A SECOND EDGE (AND STOCK WIDTH)

With the reference face and edge established, use these two surfaces to square and flatten the final two. Begin with the opposite edge and use a marking gauge to set the desired finished width of the piece. Whether it's a finished width for a cabinet part or a rough dimension for further stock processing, carefully scribe a deep line around the perimeter of the workpiece. Plane down until you hit the scribe line, thereby establishing the third flat surface. You should now have a piece that is flat on one surface and has two square, parallel edges.

STEP 4: ESTABLISH THE FINAL FACE (AND STOCK THICKNESS)

Using the first face as reference, scribe a deep line around the perimeter of the plank to establish the final desired thickness of the workpiece. Carefully plane down to the scribe line, and you'll be left with a four-sided workpiece.

STEP 5: SQUARE ONE END AND THEN THE FINISHED LENGTH

With four sides square and smooth you're ready to address the ends. Using the reference face and edge only as reference for your square, scribe a line around the workpiece and saw off the waste. Use a shooting board (see p. 178) for material 1 in. and under to clean up the sawmarks. For thicker stock like the 8/4 walnut shown here, use a low-angle block plane with the piece held vertically in a vise. That gives us five surfaces, and the sixth and last is measured to the desired length and the same steps are followed. Crosscut and handplane to clean up the sawmarks and you have six sides complete and ready for joinery.

> **TIP**
> Using the reference face and edge for all of the required joinery throughout your projects is a good habit to get into. In theory, you should be able to reference your square off any of the surfaces if you were careful in the dimensioning process. But human error can creep into the equation and small discrepancies add up along the way.

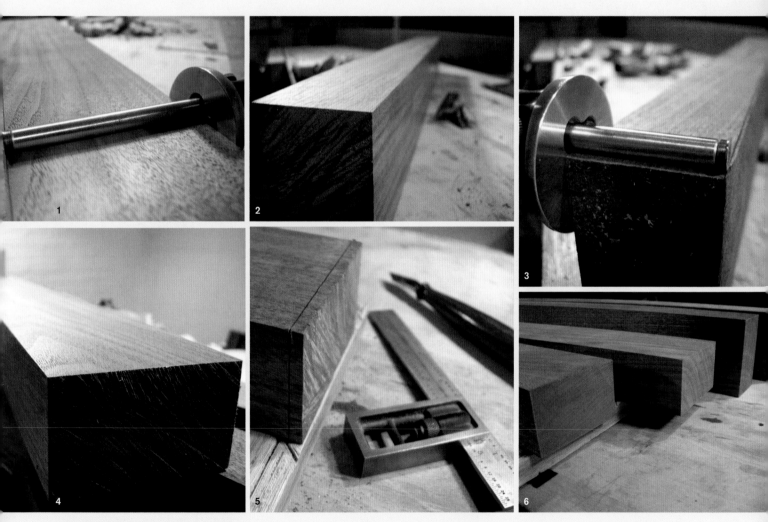

1. Use the first edge as reference to scribe the second edge. 2. The second edge is flat, square, and smooth. 3. Use the first face as reference to scribe the final face. 4. Square four sides (S4S). 5. Mark and crosscut the ends to the desired length. 6. Use a low-angle block plane to clean away the sawmarks and you're ready for joinery.

The dovetailed carcase of the card catalog (see p. 198) is a perfect example of where liquid hide glue is beneficial. With a longer open time, the assembly is much less stressful.

GLUES AND FINISHES

BEFORE BEGINNING any of the projects, I want to say a few words about the stuff that holds it all together and the finishes that'll make 'em shine.

IN PRAISE OF HIDE GLUE

I have always been attracted to hide glue for its historic qualities in traditional woodworking but also for its organic ingredients, its "friendliness" to finishes, and its reversibility. That last point is a big one and may well save *your* hide one day! I know it did mine. Even if you never make a mistake during a glue-up, the fact that the furniture we create may someday get damaged is reason enough to use this stuff. Modern glues simply don't offer the choices we have when working with hide glue.

I began using liquid hide glue as a kind of gateway into the world of these glues. I thought it would make a good

starting point before getting into the "hot stuff," and by all accounts I was correct. I purchased some of Patrick Edwards's Old Brown Glue (www.old brownglue.com). This liquid hide glue has all of the same desirable properties as hot hide glue but with a longer open time. You won't need a glue pot to store it in, and cleanup is nothing more than a bit of water. You will need to keep the glue warm while you work as well as warm it up to begin, but this routine is one that after a few days will be second nature, and the positive points of using this product far outweigh any negatives. I use liquid hide glue whenever I want a longer open time, say for dovetail joinery or for projects that involve multiple parts being glued simultaneously.

After a few months of using liquid hide glue, I purchased an electric glue pot and some high-quality hide glue.

Exercise caution if you decide to use higher gram strengths of hide glue; they may be stronger, but they have a much shorter working (or open) time, making them unsuitable for many joinery applications.

TIP

Hide glue can be purchased in different gram strengths ranging from 85 up to 315. After a bit of research, I determined that for my work and application, a gram strength of 192 would be ideal for both veneer work and furniture joinery. Some may prefer a higher gram strength of 251, which is better suited for joinery but has a shorter open time, making it less desirable for veneer work. The higher gram strengths are commonly used for instrument or model making applications. Anywhere in the range of 192 to 251 is a safe bet for furniture making. Experiment with different gram strengths and find one to your liking.

Hot hide glue comes dry in a granulated form that looks almost like oatmeal. To prepare it, you simply pour some of the dry glue into a container and cover it with fresh, cold water. Let it sit for about 20 minutes until the water has been absorbed and the granules have become a gel, again much like a prepared oatmeal. You can now add the glue to a hot glue pot and after a short time it's ready to use.

This is a simplified description of mixing and using hide glue, but it's extremely easy to work with once you

Hide glue has the consistency of prepared oatmeal after sitting for 20 minutes covered in water. At this stage it can go into the glue pot.

get started. I remember the shroud of mystery before I began using it, and it was much the same uncertainty before I started mixing my own shellac. The new recipes and formulas can be intimidating when we introduce a new product or system into our work. Trust me when I say there's nothing to worry about. If you can make oatmeal, you can mix hide glue. If it's too thick, you add some water; too thin, you add some glue. I strongly encourage you to try it, experiment with it, and use it in your own woodshop. If you'd like to learn more about the topic, Stephen A. Shepherd's *Hide Glue: Historical & Practical Applications* (Full Chisel, 2009) is an easy read that'll give you lots of information.

In summary, hide glue is easy to use; is safe for you, the environment, and your wood finishing; and has been the traditional choice of woodworkers for

1. A light coat of Tried & True varnish oil is applied to a piece of walnut. Wait an hour and wipe away the excess; repeat until you achieve the desired finish. 2. Dewaxed, super-blond shellac after 12 hours mixed with denatured alcohol. Breaking the shellac flakes into smaller pieces speeds up the dissolving process.

SHADES OF SHELLAC

SHELLAC IS SOLD in different shades, and I prefer to use a dewaxed, super-blond flake. This gives the wood a great finish without altering the natural tones in the individual species. Sometimes, when I want to attempt to blend wood tones, I'll use a dark shellac. You'll find an example of this in the card catalog project (see p. 198). I wasn't able to get all of the cabinet parts out of the same plank of walnut. In fact, some of the parts came from a bit of walnut I'd had for a number of years, while the majority came from a newer piece I had purchased specifically for the projects in this book. In an attempt to bring the two walnut species closer together visually, I used a dark garnet shellac flake.

The dark shade brought all of the walnut into the same spectrum, but, truth be told, if I had a preference, I'd use the super-blond on wood that came from the same source. That isn't always possible, and these are the things you have to deal with while building furniture. If one day I build a project and look at it and think "perfect," I'd probably never build another thing again!

literally thousands of years! Who could argue with that?

THOUGHTS ON FINISH

I try to keep finishing as simple and as green as possible. I don't enjoy working with chemicals or solvents, and I'm not set up for spraying or anything that would involve a sterile or dust-free environment. For years I've used Tried & True™ oil and varnish mixture. It's manufactured and sold by a small company in the United States (www.triedandtruewoodfinish.com), and I've never had a problem using it. It's environmentally friendly, easy to apply, and you don't have to worry about getting it on your skin. Wipe on a light coat, allow it to soak in for about an hour, and then wipe off the excess.

You can apply multiple coats, building up a sheen with each additional layer.

The more you rub the surface, the more of a sheen you'll get. For furniture applications I usually apply three to six coats, depending on the finish I'm after.

SHELLAC

As you may have guessed, I prefer using natural products in my shop, and another finish you'll see me using in the projects that follow is shellac. Now what could be more natural than that? If you don't know, shellac is a resin secreted by a lac bug. This secretion is collected and processed into dry flakes; when mixed with denatured alcohol, it becomes the liquid shellac we use in woodworking. It's also used in many other industries, from candy coatings to pharmaceutical applications. Purchase high-quality shellac flakes and mix up relatively small batches. Once mixed, shellac has a shelf life of a few months

A small ball of cheesecloth wrapped in a tightly knit fabric makes a great shellac applicator.

so, to avoid waste, mix only what you think you'll use. The mixing process is a little like the hide glue mentioned earlier. Add dry shellac flakes to a container, cover them with denatured alcohol, and wait about 24 hours until they're dissolved.

Different ratios will give you different consistencies, which are known as *the cut*. I prefer a 1-lb. to 2-lb. cut, which means the shellac is thinner and, in my opinion, easier to apply. You'll need to apply more coats, but the control you'll have while applying it trumps the extra steps involved in application.

To mix a 2-lb. cut, begin with 8 oz. of dry shellac and mix it with 32 oz.

(1 qt. U.S.) of denatured alcohol. If you'd like a thinner mix, cut down the amount of dry shellac you begin with. Most shellac flakes you purchase come with mixing instructions, and through a bit of experimenting, you'll find one that's right for you.

Shellac can be applied with a brush or you can wipe it on with an applicator, which is the method I prefer. To make the applicator, known as *a rubber*, use an egg-size ball of cheesecloth tightly wrapped in a clean cloth. Make sure the surface of the rubber is flat and smooth so you don't drag any runs while applying the finish. As you work, charge the rubber with shellac as needed.

FINAL FINISH

In closing, I usually finish my pieces with a top coat of wax. I use either a natural citrus wax or a beeswax and apply it with a 000, super-fine steel wool, which leaves a silky-smooth finish to the work. Experiment with different finishing techniques and products. Find a few methods that work for you in your shop and refine them so you can enjoy the process. I know a few woodworkers who stress so much when it comes to the finishing stages of a project. Discover what you like and do what I do: Keep it simple. Now let's go make some shavings!

The finished saw bench in cherry.

THE SAWYER'S BENCH

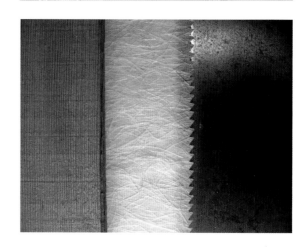

"A man who has made a
reputation for his goods knows
its value as well as its cost,
and will maintain it."

—Henry Disston

SAWYER'S BENCH

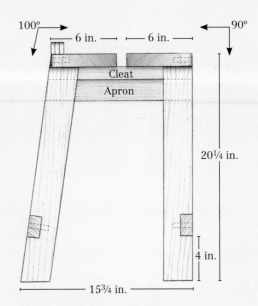

100°   6 in.   6 in.   90°

Cleat

Apron

20¼ in.

4 in.

15¾ in.

END VIEW

TOP VIEW

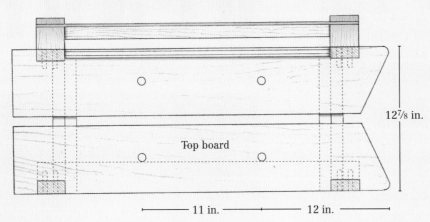

12⅞ in.

Top board

11 in.   12 in.

SIDE VIEW

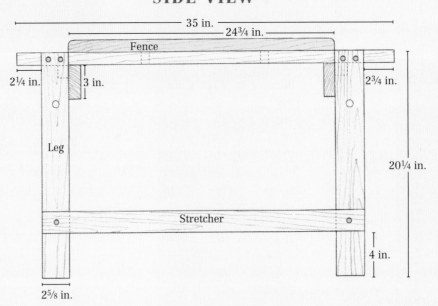

35 in.

24¾ in.

Fence

2¼ in.   3 in.   2¾ in.

Leg

20¼ in.

Stretcher

4 in.

2⅝ in.

Finished benchtop view.

THE FIRST STEP we take in any woodworking project regardless of the design or construction style is rough dimensioning material (see p. 4), and there is nowhere better suited for carrying out this task than on a dedicated saw bench.

Working wood with hand tools demands we invest a fair amount of time pushing and pulling a handsaw, so I think we owe it to ourselves to take a closer look at our sawing setup and make this affair as enjoyable and efficient as possible. The hours spent breaking down furniture components and assembling our cut lists will be much more satisfying.

The design shown here is based on a traditional saw bench shown in Bernard E. Jones's classic book *The Practical Woodworker* with a few alterations. The first and most obvious was making one side of the bench square to the top. This modification makes ripcutting much more effective without the worry of sawing into a splayed leg. (If you ever decide to use a splayed-leg design, you'd better build two benches and do your ripcutting with the board spanning between them.) Having one side square is a great

CUT·LIST

LEGS: 90° SIDE	2	1¾ IN. × 2⅝ IN. × 20¼ IN.
LEGS: 100° SIDE	2	1¾ IN. × 2⅝ IN. × 20⅝ IN.
STRETCHERS	2	1¾ IN. × 1¾ IN. × 30 IN.
TOP BOARDS	2	1 IN. × 6 IN. × 35 IN.
APRONS	2	¾ IN. × 3 IN. × 13¼ IN.
CLEATS	2	¾ IN. × 1 IN. × 9⅝ IN.
FENCE	1	¾ IN. × 1 IN. × 24¾ IN.

reference while ripping wood. Eyeing down the side will help train your eye and keep your sawcut square and true. The second improvement was adding a removable fence, which makes crosscutting more efficient without having to sacrifice your knees trying to hold stock in place when sawing.

My version of this traditional design has a benchtop made of two parallel boards, creating a ripping notch for added support when ripping narrow stock. The bird's mouth along with an array of ¾-in. holes in the top as well as in the legs makes this a versatile appliance suited to many other workshop applications. The joinery is pretty straightforward, making this a great weekend project and a perfect place to begin our unplugged journey.

These cherry planks are ready for rough dimensioning.

SELECTING MATERIALS

All of the workshop appliance projects can be made from whatever suitable material you have on hand in your shop. Take a look through your offcut pile before buying any wood and use whatever is straight and stable. Keep in mind that hardwood will withstand much more abuse, but softwoods like eastern fir or southern pine will do in a pinch.

I had some cherry left over from a past project and decided to use it for my bench. I made this same design a little over a year ago using local white ash. Both species worked well. The ash bench weighed 30 lb., while this cherry version is 20.2 lb. Here in southern Ontario, ash is about half the price of cherry.

START WITH THE LEGS AND STRETCHERS

Study the drawing on p. 14 and the cut list on p. 15 and cut all of the components to size. Flatten and square them to begin laying out the joinery.

Begin with each side assembly, made up of two legs and a cross stretcher. This is a simple lap joint that when properly executed will be strong enough for a generation of use and

1. The first two sawcuts establish the width of the lap joint. 2. Make a series of crosscuts and remove the waste with a chisel. 3. Use a router plane to fine-tune the depth.

abuse. Lay the legs flat on your workbench and place the stretcher on top where it'll be joined 4 in. up from the bottom. Scribe each side of the stretcher with a knife line and remove it. There is no measuring involved. If the stretcher is slightly wider at one end, no problem; the scribe lines should make for a perfect fit. The depth of the lap joint is half of the overall thickness of each component. I use a knife line to score crisp, deep lines around the waste areas, which will help reduce any wood tearing down beyond the marks.

Once you have the bulk of the waste removed, a router plane is great for fine-tuning the joinery. My large router plane spans the gap and rests on each side of the joint. Once I set the cutting iron, I can be sure all of the joinery will be flat and a consistent depth.

Follow this procedure for the four legs and two side stretchers and then turn your attention to the top of the legs (see the photos on p. 18). To mark the depth of the lap joint in the top of each leg, set a marking gauge using the top board as reference. Again, no measuring is required. The thickness of the top board will be exactly the depth needed for the joint. With your marking gauge set, go ahead and scribe the depth on the legs. The width is half of the leg thickness and should also be marked at this stage. Saw the notches in the top of the legs and check your joinery ("Joinery Check," below).

The two splayed legs are handled in the same way as the straight ones, except that the

➤ JOINERY CHECK ➤

Whenever you make a sawcut in any woodworking project, follow it up with a quick joinery check. Use a reliable square and make sure everything looks good. It sounds strange but I see it all the time: People saw a joint and never bother to check to see if it's square. Do this for all of your joinery. Dovetails, tenons, and, yes, even a simple lap joint. It's a good habit to get into.

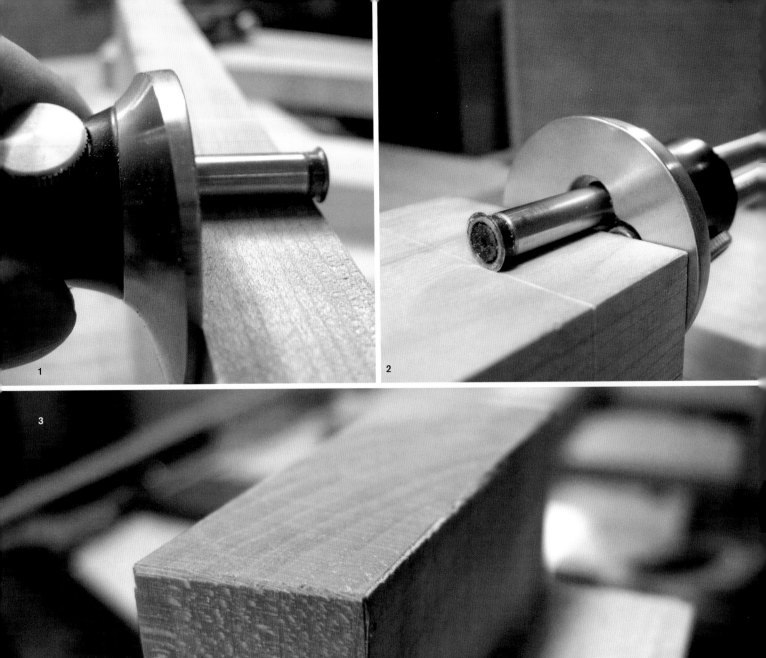

1. Set the marking gauge using the top board as reference for the lap-joint depth. 2. Transfer the line to the top of the legs. 3. Saw the square notches in the top of the legs and clean up the joinery with a sharp chisel.

1. Set a sliding bevel gauge for the top and bottom of the splayed legs. 2. Dry-fit the legs and stretchers.

Set your sliding bevel gauge to the proper angle and scribe the lines. To saw the angled cut I position the leg in my shoulder vise at the same angle as the splay. This allows me to saw straight down even though the cut is actually being made at the appropriate angle. Crosscut to remove the waste and clean everything up with a sharp chisel.

With the lap joints complete in the legs and stretchers, do a quick dry-fit to see if everything is on track. A block plane breaks the edges as I work and helps prevent chipping or blowout as I dry-fit the components.

NOTCHING THE BENCHTOP

Once all the legs are notched, transfer the widths and depths of each leg over to the benchtop boards. You shouldn't have to measure each individual leg—simply lay them in place with the stretchers dry-fit and scribe them for a perfect fit. Make sure to label the four legs and two side stretchers so you'll know which ones go where when it's time to assemble.

I follow the same procedure as when removing the waste in the top boards: Scribe the area with a knife line, saw the two sides, make a

top and bottom cuts are 10° off of 90°. Before you lay out the joinery, crosscut the legs to the desired angle. This will give you a reference face for laying out the angled lap joints.

A series of crosscuts within the width of the notch will make chopping the waste much easier.

ROUNDING THE CORNER

LEAVING SHARP EDGES and corners on furniture and workshop appliances is not a good idea. To round over a corner, first establish the curve using a divider or simply trace something in your shop with a suitable radius. Here, I used my marking gauge and traced the profile with a pencil.

Next, remove the bulk of the material with a crosscut saw. This can be done by eye. Further refine the curve with a series of paring cuts, carefully chopping down with a sharp chisel. A bench hook will save your benchtop from chisel scars, and it's always a good idea to work over a leg of your workbench for added support.

Follow with a bit more fairing with a rasp, finish off with a file, and you're done.

1. Establish the curve. 2. Crosscut to remove the bulk of the waste. 3. A paring chisel further refines the curve. 4. Almost there . . . 5. A rasp and file finish it off.

Saw the bird's mouth and round over the outside corners.

series of sawcuts across the width, and then chop out the waste.

Once you have the eight lap joints complete and you've checked them all for a dry-fit, you're pretty much ready to start thinking about assembling. Go around each piece and break the edges with a block plane. You can chamfer all of the components if you like, but I put only a slight bevel on mine.

Now's also the time to saw the bird's mouth, which is cut to approximately 65°. With the top angle established, you're left with two sharp outside corners; round them over with a saw, a chisel, and a little rasp and file work, as explained in "Rounding the Corner" on the facing page.

Bore any ¾-in. holes you may want to add for holdfasts or surface clamps and drill for the dowel holes that will hold the removable fence (see "Working with Dowel Centers" on p. 23). It's easier to do this now before everything is assembled.

Drill any holes before assembly is complete.

WORKING WITH SUBASSEMBLIES

Glue-ups in the workshop can be a real nightmare. The best way to avoid catastrophe is by subassembling project components: Don't try to glue an entire piece at once; break it down into subassemblies and save yourself the stress.

Begin with the sides and glue up the legs and stretchers (see the left photo below). I used liquid hide glue, so I let these pieces set overnight. Next, glue up the apron and leg cleats. Mark the widths of the legs in from the ends of the aprons to show where the cleats attach. The tops of the cleats and aprons should be flush. The cleats will make the assembly a little easier as they give something to reference to when assembling the bench top to the legs. Once the glue has set up, remove the clamps and plane the two components flush.

The components are now ready for final assembly. I drive wooden dowels through all of

Drive wooden dowels through the lap joints for added insurance.

the lap joints as extra insurance that they'll stay put through the years. You can make your own or use store-bought dowels like the Miller dowels shown in the photo above. The dedicated bit that comes with the Miller dowel system works well in my vintage brace and makes quick work of the holes; drive the dowels home with a bit

1. Assemble the legs and stretchers first; clamp and leave to cure overnight. 2. Plane the aprons and cleats flush when the glue is dry.

1. Drill the holes for the removable fence.

WORKING WITH DOWEL CENTERS

DOWEL CENTERS are an essential tool when you work with dowels. They take the guesswork and measuring out of finding the exact location of the holes. They're especially convenient when used for a component that needs to be removable, as for the fence for the saw bench. Start by placing the fence on the top outside edge of the splayed side of the bench and trace its location. Remove the fence and drill four ¼-in. holes in the benchtop.

Insert the dowel centers in the holes and gently line up the fence in its final position. Push down on the fence and you're left with the exact location showing where the holes in the fence need to be drilled. Drill the holes in the bottom of the fence and glue in the dowels. When the glue sets, trim the dowels to length and lightly chamfer the ends for ease of assembly and removal.

2. Dowel centers leave small dimples in the bottom of the fence to show where holes should be drilled.
3. Glue the dowels in the bottom of the fence.

1. Drill and countersink the apron and attach it to the inside of the legs with three #8 by 1½-in. wood screws.
2. The apron and leg cleat attached. 3. Scratch a decorative bead on the fence for a nice personal touch.

of glue. When the glue is dry, trim the ends with a flush-cutting saw and plane them flush to finish.

ASSEMBLING THE BENCH

With the joinery pegged, lay the top boards face down on your benchtop and attach the leg assemblies. The aprons and leg cleats come in handy to square things up, while providing a clamping surface as I drive in some stainless-steel screws to hold everything together. I don't glue the apron and cleat assembly to the legs in case I want to disassemble the bench at a later date.

At this point the saw bench is complete. You could add a bottom shelf if you'd like, but I leave that space open so it doesn't interfere with sawing through the ripping notch. One last detail I should mention is the decorative bead I scratched into the fence. This is completely unnecessary but gives a personalized touch to the finished piece. Even a workshop appliance can be made to look good and is all I needed to call this project complete.

DESIGN GALLERY

1. Two dowels through each leg's top joint. 2. The ¾-in. holes in the straight side of the bench legs are ideal for surface clamps. 3. Splayed side of bench with fence and bird's mouth detail.

One of six of our original funeral chairs in Cape Breton.
These chairs are almost 100 years old and are my inspiration …

THE FUNERAL CHAIR

"Because I could not stop for death, he kindly stopped for me."

—Emily Dickinson

FUNERAL CHAIR

BRIDLE JOINERY DETAIL

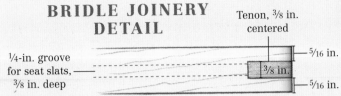

Tenon, ⅜ in. centered

¼-in. groove for seat slats, ⅜ in. deep

⅜ in.

5/16 in.

5/16 in.

SEAT SLAT (END VIEW)

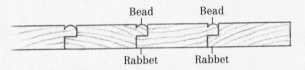

Bead

Bead

Rabbet

Rabbet

SEAT FRAME

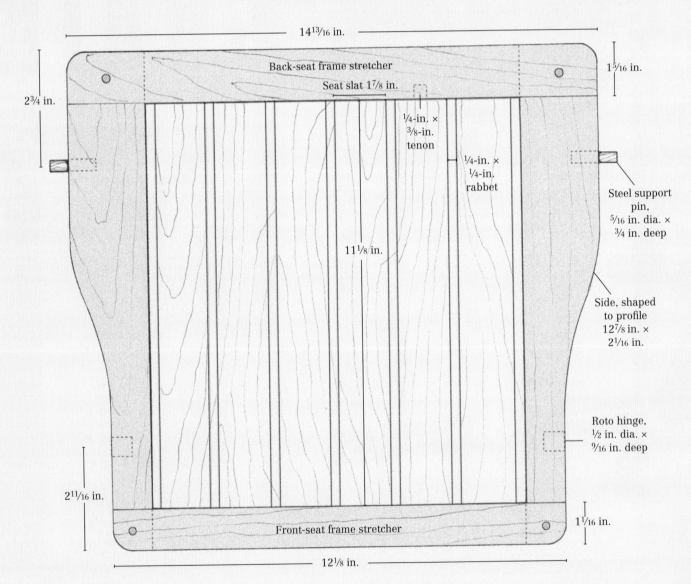

14¹³/₁₆ in.

Back-seat frame stretcher

Seat slat 1⅞ in.

1⁵/₁₆ in.

2¾ in.

¼-in. × ⅜-in. tenon

¼-in. × ¼-in. rabbet

Steel support pin, 5/16 in. dia. × ¾ in. deep

11⅛ in.

Side, shaped to profile 12⅞ in. × 2¹/₁₆ in.

Roto hinge, ½ in. dia. × 9/16 in. deep

2¹¹/₁₆ in.

Front-seat frame stretcher

1¹/₁₆ in.

12⅛ in.

MAKE ONE or build a dozen. A funeral chair is a deceptively simple, yet elegant, folding chair that's perfect for those *unexpected* gatherings. Hang a couple on a hook somewhere for a decor that screams, "Till death do us part." Of course, funerals aren't the only occasion these chairs can be used; they also come in handy for parties, weddings at home, or any other large gathering.

The nice thing about this design is that you can take some pieces of your favorite species of 4/4 hardwood (about 36 in. long), practice some rip-cutting on the new saw bench you just made (see p. 12), and you'll have the cut list assembled in no time at all. There isn't much material involved, and you should be able to put one of these together in a few days at most.

(see p. 12)

C U T . L I S T

Back legs .... 2 ......1 in. × 1½ in. × 36 in.

Front legs .... 2 ......1 in. × 1½ in. × 20½ in.

Chair back .... 1 ......¹⁵⁄₁₆ in. × 4³⁄₁₆ in. × 15¼ in.

Bottom front
stretcher .... 1 ......¹⁵⁄₃₂ in. × 1¼ in. × 16¼ in.

Back stretchers .. 2 ......⅞ in. × 1⅛ in. × 13½ in.

SEAT FRAME

Sides (shaped to
plan) .... 2 ......1 in. × 2¹⁄₁₆ in. × 12⅞ in.

Back-seat frame
stretcher .... 1 ......1 in. × 1⁵⁄₁₆ in. × 14³⁄₁₆ in.

Front-seat frame
stretcher .... 1 ......1 in. × 1¹⁄₁₆ in. × 12⅛ in.

Seat slats .... 6 ......½ in. × 1⅞ in. × 11⅛ in.

HARDWARE

Roto hinges .... 4 ......½ in. dia.

Steel rod .... 2 ......(approx.) ⁵⁄₁₆ in. dia. × 1¼ in.

… and this is my interpretation: an updated funeral chair in cherry and maple.

CHAIR FRAME

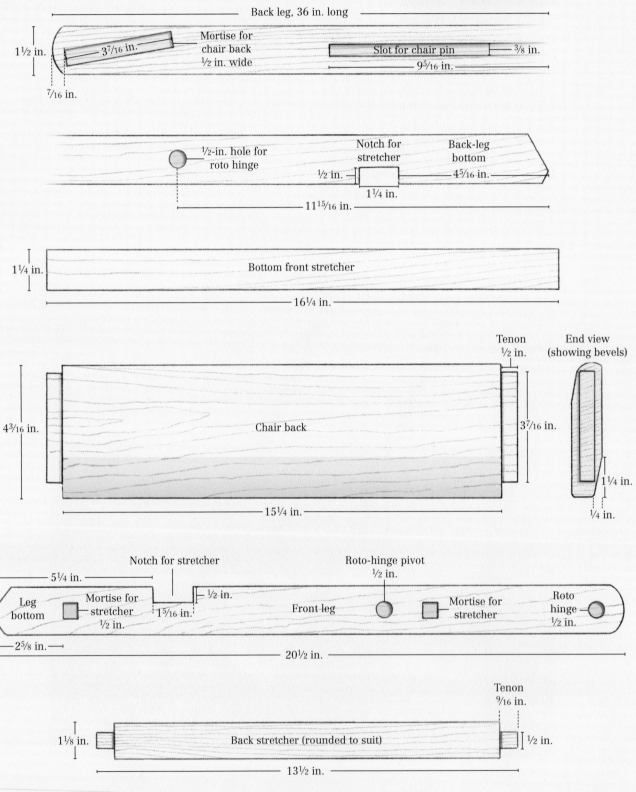

Back leg, 36 in. long

1½ in.

3⁷⁄₁₆ in.

Mortise for chair back ½ in. wide

Slot for chair pin

⅜ in.

9⁵⁄₁₆ in.

⁷⁄₁₆ in.

½-in. hole for roto hinge

Notch for stretcher

Back-leg bottom

½ in.

1¼ in.

4⁵⁄₁₆ in.

11¹⁵⁄₁₆ in.

1¼ in.

Bottom front stretcher

16¼ in.

Tenon ½ in.

End view (showing bevels)

4³⁄₁₆ in.

Chair back

3⁷⁄₁₆ in.

1¼ in.

¼ in.

15¼ in.

Notch for stretcher

Roto-hinge pivot ½ in.

5¼ in.

½ in.

1½ in.

Leg bottom

Mortise for stretcher ½ in.

1⁵⁄₁₆ in.

Front leg

Mortise for stretcher

Roto hinge ½ in.

2⅝ in.

20½ in.

Tenon ⁹⁄₁₆ in.

1⅛ in.

Back stretcher (rounded to suit)

½ in.

13½ in.

PREPARING THE STOCK

Every project begins with stock selection, and this one is no exception. For the frame, I'm using some quartersawn cherry I had on hand in my shop. Curly maple adds some nice contrast for the seat slats, but if it's not to your taste, use whatever looks good to you. Begin by ripping your rough stock to the required widths and then crosscut them to length (see the cut list on p. 29). Once you have your cut list roughed out, break out the handplanes and dimension all of the components square. The only exceptions are the two sides of the seat frame; these have a curved element but are easily shaped with a bowsaw and some spokeshave work.

START WITH THE SEAT

Working from full-scale drawings, lay out the bridle joints for the seat frame. Leave the front seat stretcher long until you've finished shaping the side pieces. While shaping the curves, it's all too easy to inadvertently take a few too many passes and make the fronts of the side members a little narrower than the plans dictate. Don't worry if you do. Just work off your

WHAT'S IN A NAME?

THE FUNERAL CHAIR. I discovered that some early religions would prepare their deceased bishops sitting upright in a "funeral chair," and there's also reference to seating arrangements during shiva, the seven-day mourning period following a burial. According to Jewish custom, mourners sit on low chairs to symbolize their awareness that life has changed and their desire to be close to the ground where the loved one was buried.

I'm not sure these low chairs are a perfect match for my funeral chair, but it's interesting to say the least. In Cape Breton, many of the older generation still refer to this style chair as a funeral chair, and in some rural areas, funerals are still held in the home. When mourners gather, the funeral chairs are brought out.

Rough-shape the sides of the seat with a bowsaw and refine the curve with a spokeshave. Full-scale drawings are essential.

finished sizes and crosscut the front stretcher to fit the overall width of the seat once you've finished shaping the frame sides.

After the chair sides are shaped and the front and back seat stretchers are crosscut to fit, lay out the bridle joints. Use a marking gauge and pencil in the waste area (see the photos on the facing page).

CUTTING THE BRIDLE JOINTS

Begin with the workpiece held vertically in your vise. The lower you set it, the more stable it will be. These are ripping cuts so a finely tuned ripsaw is important. Start your sawcut at the far end of the workpiece and try to split the scribe line.

Holding the saw with a light grip and at a forward angle to the workpiece, begin your cut using your thumb and finger as a rest for the saw plate (see the photos on p. 34).

Carefully work back across the width of the end grain, eyeing the line as you saw back toward yourself. Slowly lower the saw plate as you move across the end grain. With a little practice, you should be able to steer the saw into the exact position you want. Once you have

⊹ **KEEPING IT VERTICAL** ⊹

I've seen a lot of different techniques for hand-sawing joinery. Most require setting the workpiece at an angle in your vise and usually involve shifting the workpiece a number of times during the procedure. This method never really worked for me, and I find that starting with the workpiece vertical is a slightly faster approach. It works for me, so why not give it a try?

TIP

Scribe the bridle joints on the seat frame parts.

a kerf established across the end grain, you can concentrate on the vertical line closest to you.

Begin to angle the saw upward and start sawing down the edge of the workpiece, being careful not to lift the saw out of the top kerf as you go. Eyeing the scribe line, continue tilting the saw until you reach the baseline. As you make the vertical cut, you'll find the saw will continue to follow the top kerf you already established.

Once you reach the bottom shoulder scribe line, you can now concentrate on finishing the cut. The two kerfs will guide the saw plate and all you'll have to worry about is the depth on the opposite side. Work slowly down and eye over the top as you approach horizontal in the sawcut. You'll notice in the photos on p. 34 that even though my thumb is no longer guiding the saw plate, I maintain contact with the workpiece as I go. This somehow allows me to "feel" the cut as I work and gives me a better sense of plumb while I saw.

Because these are bridle joints, the waste still needs to be removed on the other half of the

joint. Depending on the scale of the work, I'll either use a fretsaw, for small-scale parts, or a bowsaw for larger joinery in the 2-in. thickness range. For this funeral chair, the fretsaw will suffice. Drop the fretsaw blade down into the ripsaw kerf and saw away the waste.

With the rip cuts complete and the waste removed, the shoulder cuts follow the same basic procedure. Working off a bench hook, I begin the kerf on the far side of the workpiece. Slowly drop the saw plate down as you establish the kerf across the width of the piece. Once the kerf

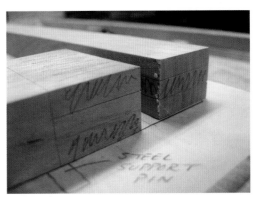

Pencil in the waste side of each joint as you go.

1. Begin the cut on the far side of the workpiece, with the saw angled downward. 2. Lower the saw into the workpiece. 3. Angle the saw upward and saw down the front edge. 4. Continue tilting the saw until you reach the baseline. 5. Bring the saw horizontal to finish the cut. 6. The finished vertical cuts.

Use a fretsaw to cut the other half of the bridle joint and clean up the waste left at the bottom of the joint with a chisel.

is splitting the scribe line, you can concentrate on the vertical cut to establish the shoulder. Once the bridle joinery is complete, test-fit the seat frame parts.

PLOWING THE GROOVE FOR THE SEAT SLATS

Once you're happy with the bridle joints, move on to the $3/8$-in.-deep groove that the seat-slat tenons fit into on the inside of the front and back seat stretchers. The groove will land inside the existing bridle joint so you don't have to worry about it showing in the end grain when complete. I use a small plow plane fitted with a $1/4$-in. iron to cut the groove (see the top photo on p. 36).

DRILL THE ROTO HINGE AND SUPPORT PIN HOLES

The next step is to mark and drill the holes in the seat sides for the Roto hinges and the seat support pins.

The steel rod I used for the support pins is $5/16$ in. dia. Feel free to use whatever you have that's similar in diameter; I wouldn't go as

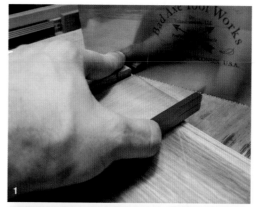

Cut the shoulders with a similar technique, beginning on the far side of the workpiece and dropping the saw horizontal to finish the cut.

The seat-slat tenon groove falls inside the existing bridle joints.

Scribe the sides of the groove with a cutting gauge before you begin plowing out the waste. You'll get cleaner edges that way.

light as ¼ in. nor would I go over ½ in. dia. Whatever size rod you use, make sure the slots in the rear chair legs are made to match! Refer to the drawing on p. 28 for their exact locations. Clamp the parts and mark them out together for continuity sake.

CHAIR-FRAME JOINERY

My antique version of a funeral chair is held together with simple butt joints, dowels, and wood screws. One could argue that these are sufficient (and our set of six have certainly proven that through the years), but because this is a project to develop our joinery skills, I've beefed things up a little with some mortise-and-tenon joinery and half laps as well as the bridle joints we used for the seat frame.

Begin with the two back legs and lay out the top angled mortise locations for the chair-back tenons. A paper template will make this step easier. Draw a full-scale mock-up on some trac-

1. A small square set on the workpiece helps maintain square as you drill. 2. The $^5/_{16}$-in. holes for the support pins and the $^1/_2$-in. holes for the Roto hinges complete in the sides of the seat frame.

ing paper and transfer the corner locations of the mortises through the paper template with an awl (see the top left photo on p. 38). With the corners clearly marked, pencil in the perimeter and then knife in some scribe lines. Use a $^1/_2$-in. bit to remove the bulk of the material and then square the mortise with some chisel work.

Moving down the back legs, mark the pivot locations for the Roto hinges and the slot for the chair support pins. The slot is basically a long mortise, and my brace and bit quickly removes the bulk of the material. Refine the sides with a chisel and finish off the depth of the slot with a router plane. Drill the holes for the Roto hinges using a $^1/_2$-in. bit to a depth of $^9/_{16}$ in.

Still working on the back legs, next scribe and cut the lower notch for the bottom front stretcher (see the top photo on p. 39). Make a series of crosscuts to define the waste area and clean up the joint with a chisel. Chop in from one side, stopping about halfway through. There's less risk of blowing out material on the opposite edge that way. Turn the piece and finish removing the material from the opposite side. Test-fit the lower stretcher after the notches are cut. Creep up on this fit; if the stretcher is too wide, instead of trying to make the notch wider, take a light pass off the stretcher with a handplane until you achieve a perfect fit.

The shorter front legs are next and receive the same treatment. Mark the pivot locations for the Roto hinges and the two rear stretcher

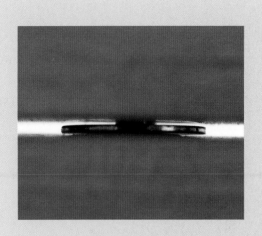

ROTO HINGES

I DISCOVERED Roto hinges about 10 years ago when making a small project for my home in Cape Breton. They are extremely handy in all sorts of applications where a pivot joint is required. The hinges are quick and easy to install and come in a range of sizes (I purchase mine from Lee Valley Tools®; item #00S01.03). Drill a hole, spread a bit of glue, and lightly tap the hinge into place.

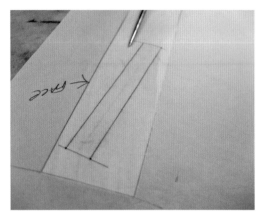

Why mess about with difficult angle settings and rulers? It's a lot easier to draw a full-scale plan on some tracing paper and transfer your lines.

I can't imagine why some woodworkers choose to chop mortises using only a chisel. Though both methods are fine, the brace and bit makes quicker work of the process.

mortise locations (see the center photo on p. 39). These are ½-in. squared mortises, ⅝ in. deep. I kept the joinery sizes pretty consistent for this project and, with only a handful of tool sizes, you'll have the main joinery complete in no time at all.

CUTTING THE CHAIR BACK AND STRETCHER TENONS

After the leg joinery is complete, the chair back and two leg stretcher tenons are next. Working off the drawing on p. 30, lay out the tenons and saw them following the same basic sawing rules we covered earlier (see the bottom photos on p. 39). Dry-fit the parts as you go.

1. Rough-out the slot for the chair support pins with a brace and bit. 2. Define the sides of the slot with a chisel. 3. A large router plane is the ideal tool for refining the depth of the slot.

Cut the notch for the lower front stretcher.

Mark the locations for the stretcher mortises on the front legs.

A good-fitting mortise-and-tenon joint should go together with hand pressure only, but not be loose enough to fall out once assembled dry. Practice cutting joinery before you undertake any project; it helps.

TIP

FINAL-SHAPING THE STRETCHERS AND CHAIR BACK

You can leave the stretchers square with a nice chamfer on the edges, but I decided to take these stretchers a step further and round them into an oval shape along their length. Using two elevated benchdogs (see p. 40), begin by planing down each corner to create an octagon shape. As you work your way around the stretcher a few times, the oval profile starts to take shape.

The chair back requires a large chamfer on the top front and bottom back to fit within the width of the rear legs. Using a combination square, set some guide lines and chamfer down the profile. The top width of the chamfer is marked ¼ in. from the edges, while the depth is 1¼ in. down (see the drawing on p. 30).

1. For the tenons on the back leg stretchers, rip the four cheek cuts while the piece is held vertically in a vise and then move to the bench hook to complete the shoulder cuts. 2. After the shoulder cuts are made, use a chisel to refine the baselines; then dry-fit the parts.

ELEVATED BENCH DOGS

I USE THESE ELEVATED BENCH-DOGS to hold work up off the benchtop. They fit my existing benchdog holes and raise the workpiece, which makes it easier to shape cabinet and chair parts with a handplane or spokeshave. Refer to the drawing below and lay out the shapes of the two dogs. I'm using 4/4 maple for mine. Saw the shapes and clean up the edges. Fine tune the bottom tenon area so they fit snugly into your existing bench holes. If your bench has round dog holes, then round this bottom area to match. Drill pilot holes through the top section of the dogs and insert screws. Place one dog in the bench top and the other in your shoulder vise and clamp the work piece between. The screws protrude just enough to slightly pierce the work as the shoulder vise is tightened.

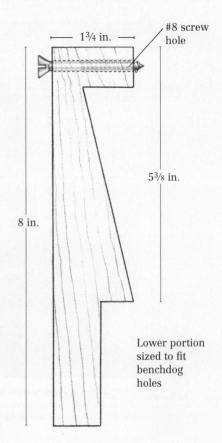

#8 screw hole

1¾ in.

5⅜ in.

8 in.

Lower portion sized to fit benchdog holes

1. Elevated benchdogs make rounding stock easy. 2. Lay out the dog profiles using an existing benchdog as reference. 3. Saw the shapes and predrill screw holes. 4. The dogs make the process of rounding furniture parts easy and enjoyable. 5. Detail showing screw in benchdog head.

1. Beginning with each corner, plane down until you achieve the desired shape. 2. A bit of fine sanding will knock off the facets and bring the oval closer to round. It doesn't have to be perfect.

FINAL-SHAPING THE TOPS AND BOTTOMS OF THE LEGS

With all of the chair joinery complete, shape the tops of the legs and cut the bottoms as indicated in the drawing on p. 30. To create the round tops, make a series of sawcuts on a bench hook to rough-out the basic shape. Follow with some paring work to refine the curve. Refine and blend the leg top with a file and finally a bit of fine sandpaper.

Next, lay out the angled cuts for the leg bottoms as shown in the photo on p. 42. Back at the bench hook, make the crosscuts on each leg bottom and slightly bevel the edges with a block plane.

1. Begin removing the waste from the chair back with a jack plane and creep up to the lines with a low-angle block plane. Finish by rounding the outside edge slightly. 2. Dry-fit the chair back mortise-and-tenon joinery. 3. Rough-shape the round profiles on the tops of the legs using the bench hook and crosscut saw.

For controlled paring cuts with a chisel, hold the chisel end with a finger wrapped around it and the rest of your hand balanced on the workpiece. Use your shoulder to push the chisel down through the end grain. Make sure your chisels are sharp and you'll have no problem executing a fine curve using this method.

MAKING THE SEAT SLATS

With the legs shaped and the main frame joinery complete, the next step is to make the slats for the seat. In the six chairs that make up my original set, the seat slats were cut to the shape of the seat and screwed directly to the top of the seat frame (see the photo on pp. 26–27) Adding the groove in the seat frame updates the design and gives us a few more options for joinery.

The slats fit in the groove and need room for seasonal movement. I measured the overall width of the inside of the chair seat and decided that six slats at 1⅞ in. wide, with a ¼-in. shiplap, will fill the area and allow for ⅛ in. of space on both sides for any expansion.

Begin by roughing-out your stock (I used curly maple) and fine-tune the length on a shooting board. Next, set up to cut the ¼-in.-deep rabbets in each of the slats. The outside of the two end slats don't need a rabbet, but

Use a sliding bevel gauge to lay out the bottom of the legs.

1. You'll cut five pairs of mating rabbets; the outside edges of the end slats are not rabbeted. 2. As an optional detail, scratch a bead down the top edge of the seat slats. 3. On a bench hook, crosscut the tenon shoulders and then rip away the cheeks with the slats held vertically in your vise. 4. The 1/8-in. gap on the outside edges of the slats is for seasonal wood movement.

the insides and the middle slats do. Each slat gets a rabbet down the bottom edge of one side and the top edge of the other to create the shiplap effect we're after. I cut the rabbets with a rabbet plane and fine-tuned the fit with a shoulder plane.

You can leave the slats as is or lightly chamfer the edges. I chose to scratch a bead down the top edges, which will help conceal any small openings that may occur during seasonal wood movement. The slat on the far right side receives a bead on each edge, while the rest need one only down the left side.

The groove we cut in the seat frame earlier is 1/4 in. wide and 3/8 in. deep. The tenons on the ends of the slats need to mate with the groove, so scribe the ends and cut them next. Follow this same procedure for all six slats and dry-fit the seat components.

PREFINISHING THE PARTS

On a project like this, it's much easier to prefinish the parts while everything is still separate. I'm using Tried & True oil/varnish mixture (see p. 10), which will be easy to maintain yet durable for many years of use. This oil/varnish is easy to apply: Simply wipe it on, wait an hour, and wipe off any excess. Repeat

Prefinish the chair parts with an oil/varnish before any gluing is done.

Cut the ⁵⁄₁₆-in. steel rod for the seat support pins.

Dry-fitting the assembly is an important step to take before you commit to glue. If any problems arise? Well, I hope you use hot hide glue as I do: it's reversible!

as desired until the finish is to your liking; the more you rub this stuff, the brighter it gets. I stopped at three coats.

I like to let the finish sit overnight before continuing on with the glue-up. This is a good time to assemble your hardware and, if you haven't yet, cut the steel rod to 1¼-in. lengths for the seat support pins. I attach a small metal vise to my benchtop and use a hacksaw to make quick work of the pins. Chamfer any sharp edges with a metal file.

GLUING UP THE CHAIR

The glue-up has to happen in stages as one section nests inside the next. The seat frame is glued first and then this assembly is glued into the front leg assembly. Once that has time to cure, the seat and front leg assembly is glued into the back legs to finish. You'll see what I mean as we go along.

THE SEAT ASSEMBLY

Glue up the seat assembly to begin. Place two ⅛-in. shims between the slats and the frame so the seat slats remain centered in the seat frame until everything has cured. Apply only a minimal amount of glue to the slats, just so

Reinforce the bridle joints at the corners of the seat frame with dowels. Saw the dowels flush and clean up with a sharp chisel.

A good-fitting bridle joint has plenty of long-grain glue surface and will stay together through many years of use, but I like to reinforce the joints with dowels, both for added insurance and as a decorative touch. Drill and drive some wooden dowels down through the bridle joints while the seat is still in the clamps. I use Miller dowels as they're convenient and easy to work with. The stepped drill bits fit nicely in my vintage brace, and they're available in a variety of wood species and sizes. Trim the dowels with a flush-cutting saw and finish with a sharp chisel to bring everything flush.

Once the dowels are trimmed and the clamps are removed, round the corners of the chair seat. Mark the area and follow the same procedure as for rounding the leg tops described earlier. A few crosscuts establish the basic shape and some paring work with a

they'll stay together as you work. The slats are not glued to the seat frame but only pressure fit and allowed to float.

Glue up the seat frame to begin the process.

1. Glue and clamp the chair back to the back legs with the seat and front leg assembly sandwiched between them. 2. Glue up the front leg assembly with the seat frame inserted between.

chisel fairs the curve. Refine the line with a fine rasp or file and touch up the area with some oil/varnish.

THE LEG ASSEMBLIES

Now move onto the front leg assembly. Glue the Roto hinges and the support pins into the chair sides and then clamp the front legs (with the front stretchers) to the seat.

After the glue has cured, you're ready for the final stage of the glue-up: the back leg assembly. Again, start by gluing the Roto hinges into place and sandwich the front leg/seat assembly between the back legs. The chair back is also glued at this time as well as the lower front stretcher.

> I decided to dowel the rest of the joinery as I did with the seat frame. If you like this option, drill and drive the dowels through the holes while the glue sets and the assemblies are still under clamp pressure. Trim with a flush-cutting saw and refine with a chisel.
>
> **TIP**

When the clamps are removed, lay the chair flat on your workbench and make sure everything is moving as it should. The beauty of this design is that the chair can be stored completely flat or hung on a wall.

Fold the chair flat on the workbench...and open on the bench to make sure the hinges are all working as they should.

DESIGN GALLERY

1. Side by side.
Which do you prefer?
2. Bridle joint detail.
3. Leather seat detail.

LEATHER-SEAT VARIATION

THE CHERRY and maple version of the funeral chair is the second I've made. The first one was made of mahogany and the seat was made from $\frac{1}{8}$-in. leather. If you'd like to try the leather-seat option, here's how. The seat is the only difference between the two chairs other than some slight shaping on some of the parts.

CUTTING THE RABBET

After the seat-frame parts are shaped and the bridle joinery is fit, scribe a line around the inside perimeter of the seat about $\frac{1}{2}$ in. in from the outside edge. Follow the overall shape of the seat frame, including the round areas on the side members. This inside area will be removed to $\frac{1}{8}$ in. in depth to create a kind of shaped rabbet around the inside of the seat frame. The $\frac{1}{8}$-in. leather will be fitted and attached here. Using a marking knife, scribe deep lines and remove the waste with a router plane and chisel. The radius of the corners is defined with a matching gouge. In this version there is no need for the seat slat grooves, but I suppose that is stating the obvious!

MAKING A TEMPLATE

The next step is to make a template for the leather seat. Make the template on tracing paper first and then, once you've made any necessary adjustments, produce a heavier card stock pattern. The pattern is made slightly smaller than the actual opening because the leather has a bit of stretch

1. Scribe a deep scribe line on the seat frame parts to establish the area to remove. 2. Use a gouge to define the radius of the corners. 3. Create the $\frac{1}{8}$-in. rabbet using a router plane and chisel.

Fit the paper template into the chair seat recess.

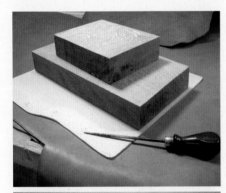

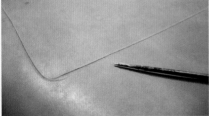

Weight the card stock pattern with oak blocks to make sure it will stay put while you scribe the shape with an awl.

to it, about $\frac{1}{16}$ in. all around seems to work.

FITTING THE LEATHER

Cut out the leather with a sharp knife and burnish the edges with a sanding block. Then follow with a good rub all over with beeswax. The wax softens as well as protects the leather while giving it a deeper sheen, which seems to match the oiled mahogany chair frame a little better.

Stretch the leather into position and hold it in place with brass furniture tacks spaced about $1\frac{1}{2}$ in. around the perimeter. You may need an extra set of hands while nailing in the tacks as you attempt to stretch the leather into place. If you're left with a small gap ($\frac{1}{16}$ in.) around the edges, don't sweat it.

The leather seat is extremely comfortable, but for my taste, I like the slightly more contemporary look of the curly maple slats on the cherry frame. That's just my opinion and I hope you trust in yours when you build your own version of the funeral chair.

Leather and mahogany funeral chair seat detail.

THE ARCHITECT'S TABLE

"Form follows function—that has been misunderstood. Form and function should be one, joined in a spiritual union."

—Frank Lloyd Wright

ARCHITECT'S TABLE

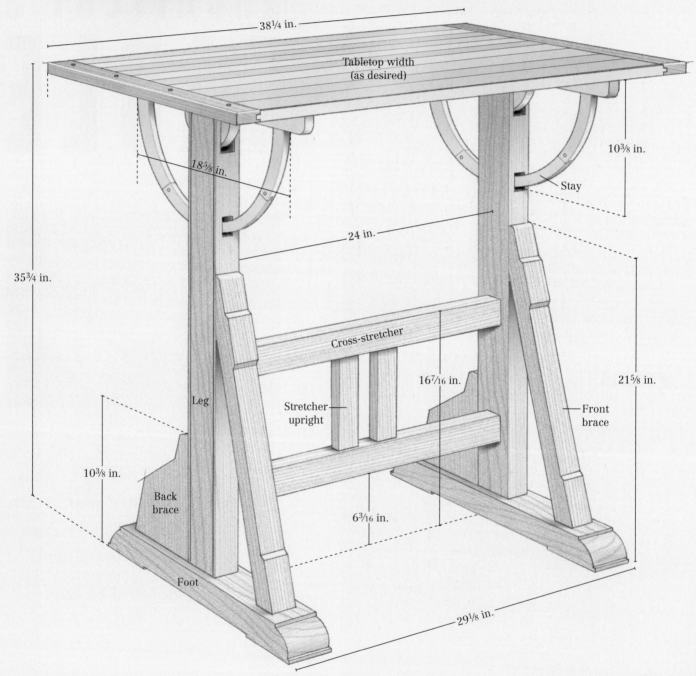

38¼ in.

Tabletop width
(as desired)

10⅜ in.

Stay

18⅝ in.

35¾ in.

24 in.

21⅝ in.

Cross-stretcher

16⁷⁄₁₆ in.

Leg

Stretcher
upright

Front
brace

10⅜ in.

Back
brace

6³⁄₁₆ in.

Foot

29⅛ in.

As utilitarian or aesthetically pleasing as you like.

THE ARCHITECT'S TABLE, also known as an architect's desk, a drawing board, or a drawing table, is a multipurpose design that can be used for large-format sketching, drawing, writing, and, of course, drafting. Over the years, I've come across a number of wonderful historical examples, including a behemoth of a table that used to reside in an industrial loft on the west side of Toronto that two close friends of mine were renting. It must have weighed hundreds of pounds and still had all of its original metal hardware working.

The version we'll be building here won't be quite as massive, but it will serve equally well as a standing desk in the workshop, a gardener's bench, a salvaged-style desk for the study, or a table in the modern office, where a vintage style is appropriate, if not downright fashionable.

CUT·LIST

FEET	2	1⅞ IN. × 3¼ IN. × 23¾ IN.
LEGS	2	1⅞ IN. × 3⁷⁄₁₆ IN. × 33 IN.
FRONT BRACES	2	1¹³⁄₁₆ IN. × 2¼ IN. × 22 IN.
BACK BRACES	2	1¹³⁄₁₆ IN. × 8½ IN. × 9 IN.
CROSS-STRETCHERS	2	1⅝ IN. × 1⅞ IN. × 26 IN.
STRETCHER UPRIGHTS	2	1⅞ IN. × 1¾ IN. × 7⅞ IN.

STAYS .... 2 .... MADE FROM THREE PIECES EACH:

ENDS (WITH TENONS)	2	1 IN. × 2½ IN. × 8½ IN.
MIDDLE	1	1 IN. × 3½ IN. × 11¼ IN.

TABLETOP SUPPORTS	2	1 IN. × 4 IN. × 23 IN.
TABLETOP CROSS-MEMBERS	2	1 IN. × 1⅛ IN. × 26½ IN.

TABLETOP

TOP LAMINATES	24 STRIPS	1⅛ IN. × 1 IN. × 37 IN.
BREADBOARD ENDS	2	1⅛ IN. × 1⅞ IN. × 23⅝ IN.

The table features solid mortise-and-tenon joinery with carefully formed stays, allowing the tabletop to tilt and lock at various angles. These wooden stays replace the traditional metal hardware often found on antique drafting tables. The tabletop uses a lamination process to highlight the edge grain of the material, but, more important, it makes a more stable work top. Breadboard ends finish off the details. Let's get started.

STOCK SELECTION

The first step in any project is to choose the wood species and determine if it needs to be specific to the design. Furniture makers and designers use specific wood for reasons of structural integrity, function, durability, and aesthetics. I chose walnut for this project simply because I had a nice plank of well-seasoned 8/4 stock in my shop. Truth be told, walnut is a great hardwood for furniture making; it will stand up to years of use, it works really well with hand tools, and it looks great too! Quartersawn oak would also work well, as would any of the cherries or maples. I would

Mark out the components on a rough plank (here, 8/4 walnut).

stay away from softwoods for a piece like this that has moving parts and round components. The stays should definitely be made from a hardwood, like maple or oak.

Start by examining the planks for ideas and clues of where to take the assortment of parts needed for the table frame. Where does the grain look the best? Are there any obvious problem areas? Will you get all of the parts from one plank? That last one's an important question to answer pretty early on. The dimensions of the parts are fairly large so there is a good deal of sawing to do.

ROUGH DIMENSIONING THE BASE COMPONENTS

Lay out the components and saw them to shape. I switch between different handsaws, depending on the part of the plank I'm saw-

The leg components, roughsawn and ready for further dimensioning.

ing; different saws for change in length, tooth geometry, or tote size are nice to have on hand.

Rough dimensioning the cut list isn't a race; it just became that way through someone else's revolution. What it is, is a healthy lifestyle choice. Think of it as the morning workout. That's about how long it took me to break

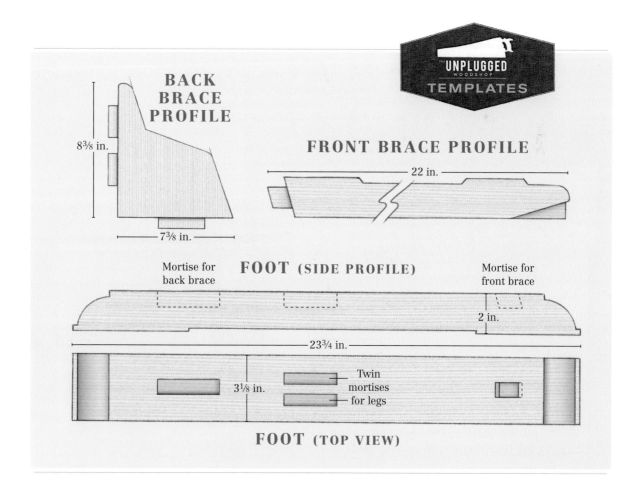

BACK BRACE PROFILE

8⅜ in.

7⅜ in.

FRONT BRACE PROFILE

22 in.

FOOT (SIDE PROFILE)

Mortise for back brace

Mortise for front brace

2 in.

23¾ in.

3⅛ in.

Twin mortises for legs

FOOT (TOP VIEW)

SOME THOUGHTS ABOUT HAND-SAWING

MAINTAINING a square cut is one of the key skills to master when you first start rip-cutting, and one of the best ways to keep your saw tracking to a line is to build yourself a sawyer's bench (see p. 12). For years I used a saw bench with four splayed legs on both sides, and I would always find that my ripcuts would drift out of plum. But once I switched to the sawyer's bench with its 90° side, my sawing accuracy immediately improved.

Another trick I've discovered along the way is to vary the sawing angle, especially on stock over 5/4 thick. Start sawing at an optimal angle of around 60° for a ripcut and 45° for a crosscut; every 8 to 10 strokes quickly lower the saw down to about 25° for a stroke or two and then raise it back up to the desired pitch. This helps you maintain a more accurate cut. When you drop the saw, you'll be inadvertently clearing a small kerf behind your saw plate, thus creating the path of least resistance as you saw along

the length of a board. Try practicing this technique a little after you get comfortable with a basic rip-cutting motion, and soon you'll forget you're even doing it and you'll be consistently sawing to a line in no time at all!

For longer cuts, one other trick is to rotate between a one-handed, pistol grip and a two-handed grip. You'll also be able to adjust and change your body position slightly to share the physical strain of heavy sawing. A one-handed grip means you're usually bent farther over the workpiece, while with a two-handed grip you can be closer to an upright stance.

These are the nuances that start occurring when you use a handsaw to rough-dimension large amounts of stock. Skills will be nourished as you put in some time on the handsaw and the saw bench, and you'll soon find that this amount of rough sawing really isn't all that difficult.

---

down the walnut components for the legs, braces, and cross-stretchers for this project. Basically, I used the entire plank of 2-in. by 13-in. by 8-ft.-long, roughsawn walnut. Make sure you're up to the challenge. You can break out one part at a time and spread the workload over a week if that works for you. Remember, it isn't a race. You may even break a sweat— I know I did! Work at a comfortable pace, and enjoy the process.

I try to leave about ¼ in. of extra material before further dimensioning. Use your own judgment and remember that the cut lists are "just" the joinery, with no extra. If the stock you're working is really twisted or there are

My go-to ripsaw is an antique 26-in. Disston D-8. It belonged to my late-granduncle Johnny Pier, who carved his name into all of his tools back in the day.

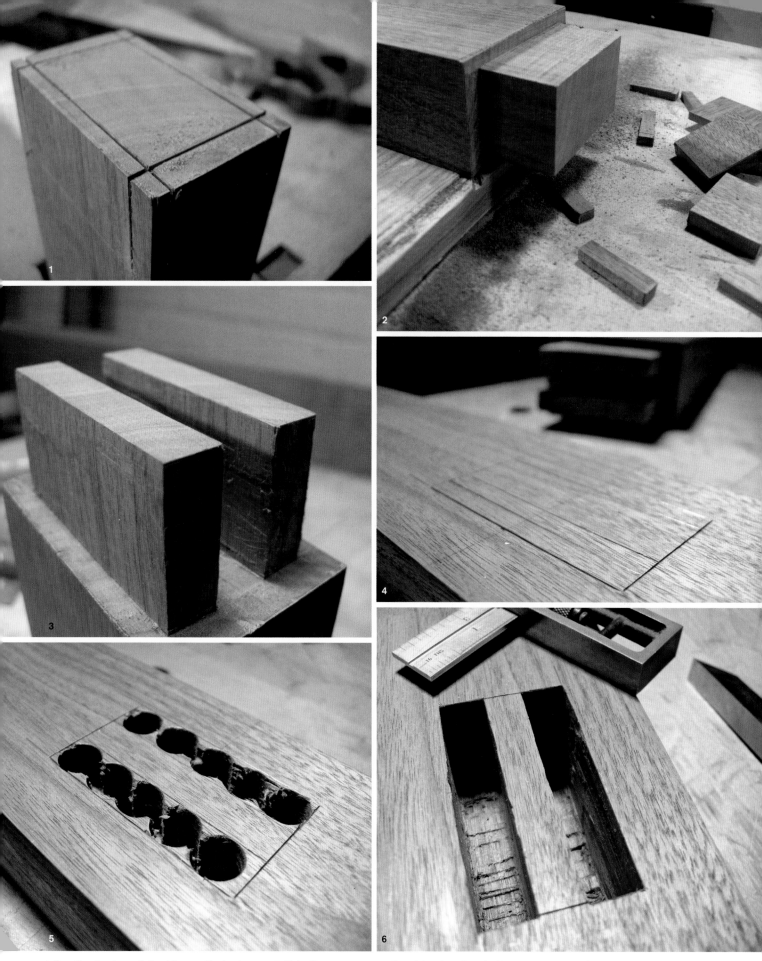

1. Saw the cheeks and shoulders on the leg tenons. 2. Make the crosscuts on a bench hook. 3. Saw the large tenon into two ¼-in. tenons and remove the waste with a bowsaw. 4. Lay out the double mortise in the feet. 5. Remove the bulk of the waste with a brace and bit. 6. Square the mortises with a chisel.

1. After rough-sawing the angled brace tenons, clean up the inside shoulders with a chisel. 2. A sliding bevel gauge is helpful for referencing the angle while you bore out the waste in the angled mortise in the feet.

many knots present, leave a little more than ¼ in. of waste, depending on the quality of the wood. There's no sense leaving more than you have to—you'll only have more sweeping to do!

Keep the joinery in mind and trace out some full-size templates of the foot, leg, and substructure components (see the drawing on p. 55). Remember to take the tenons into account when laying out the templates and the parts.

HEEL TO HEEL AND TOE FOR TOE

With the table base components roughsawn and dimensioned according to the cut list, the next step is to lay out the bottom joinery for the legs. The legs are attached to the feet using twin tenons. Anytime a large mortise-and-tenon joint is used in midsize furniture applications, it's best to break the tenon into two smaller ones. This gives more surface for gluing and makes a stronger joint.

Saw the shoulders and cheeks, and remove the bulk of the waste between the twin tenons with a fretsaw or bowsaw. Carefully pare down to the baselines with a freshly sharpened chisel. Next, lay out the mortises. Use a brace and bit to remove the bulk of the waste and

clean up the edges with a chisel, as shown in the photos on p. 57.

The shorter back braces are attached down into the foot with one wide tenon and two shorter ones into the leg. The longer angled front brace is joined with a single, angled tenon down into the foot. Refer to "Templates" on p. 55 and lay out the joinery.

Use a spokeshave to clean up the sawmarks and refine the profile of the braces.

Whenever I make mortises, I use an auger bit in my brace to remove the bulk of the material. For these angled mortises, set a sliding bevel gauge to the same angle as the brace and reference it while boring out the material (see photo 2 on the facing page). The mortise is easily squared up with a bench chisel afterward.

The next step is straightforward: cutting the shorter, back brace mortise and tenons. The bottom tenon is fairly wide and runs across the long grain of the foot; make this mortise a little longer than needed to allow for any wood movement across the width of these braces.

Dry-fit the legs with the front and back braces in place. The back braces need to mate with the legs before they're lowered down onto the feet. Fit them to the legs first and then fit the assembly to the feet. Once the legs and back braces are in place, dry-fit the long angled braces. After this first (of many) dry fits, you're ready to shape the braces. Working from full-size templates, trace the shapes onto the workpieces. Rough-shape the long brace

1. Saw the profile on the front of the feet. **2.** The profiles on the toes are roughed-out quickly with a bowsaw and then some quick paring cuts with a chisel. I like them like this.

The upper, long sloping tenons on the front angled braces that join the legs should be laid out carefully. To make it a little easier to saw this joint, scribe the shoulder lines and then use a chisel to make a shallow groove along the scribe lines. This will create a small notch that will guide your backsaw while you saw the joint. After you've made the angled shoulder cuts, rip the cheeks and saw the tenons to length.

A dry-fit.

1. Make a template and trace the shape on the top of each leg. 2. After sawing off the waste, use a rasp, file, and eventually sandpaper to finish off the leg top profiles.

with a bowsaw and clean it up with a spoke-shave, card scraper, and then some sandpaper if still needed (see the bottom photo on p. 58). The back brace is more manageable and can be easily shaped with a few sawcuts and then finished with a card scraper. Before you dry-fit everything again, rough-shape the feet using a bowsaw, chisels, rasps, files, and card scrapers (whatever it takes!).

CUTTING THE LEG TO STAY JOINERY

With the leg and brace joinery complete, cut the through mortises in the legs for the tabletop stays. Then cut the bridle joint at the top of the legs where the tabletop supports attach.

The through mortises should be marked and scribed from both sides. Use a brace and bit and bore in from one side, stopping about halfway through the leg, and then turn the piece and bore in from the other side to finish. Square up the through mortise with a chisel. I pared the through mortise down on an angle from both sides, meeting somewhere in the middle. This creates a V in the bottom of the through mortise, which allows more room for the arc of the stay to swing through.

After scribing the lines, saw the two sides of the leg-top bridle joints. Again, use a bowsaw to remove the waste material and clean up the bottom of the joint with a chisel. If you don't have a bowsaw, you could chop all of the material away with a chisel after making the ripcuts in the end grain. The bowsaw simply makes the process a little faster.

Now shape the top of the legs. I made a simple card stock template and drew in the half-round leg tops (see photo 1 on the facing page). A quick series of angled crosscuts on a bench hook, followed by some rasp and file work, finishes the leg top profiles.

If you prefer, shape the top of the legs and then saw the joinery. The reverse order worked for me, but do whichever you feel is easier.

TIP

MAKING THE TABLE SUPPORTS AND STAYS

The supports and stays are what separate this table both aesthetically and structurally from a desk or writing table. The half-round stays that pass through the legs give the piece a sense of style and utility. Traditional drafting tables had metal hardware but for this design some 4/4 maple and solid joinery will do just fine.

To begin, make full-size drawings of the top supports and stays and carefully pencil in all of the joinery. For full-size drawings with round components, you don't need to run out and purchase any large-scale drafting tools. An offcut with a hole drilled in one end, fit for a pencil, and a small finish nail inverted and inserted at the desired mid-location, pivot point makes for a simple, yet effective drawing tool (see the photo at right).

After the full-size drawing is complete, transfer the lines over to your stock, including the joinery details. I used some heavy 4/4 curly maple for these components. I'd discourage you from cutting the full profile from one wide board because the ends of the stays would be

short grain and weak. Making the stays out of three separate parts and orienting the grain so it runs the length of each section make for stronger working components.

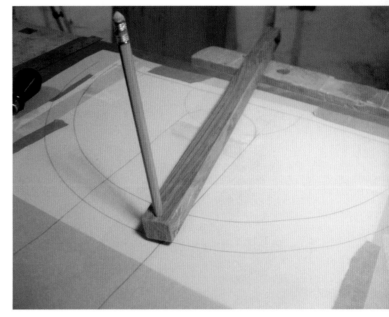

No fancy trammel points or beam compass here. An offcut with a pencil hole and a finish nail will suffice for drawing the top supports and stays.

Use carbon tracing paper to transfer the full-size drawings onto the stock.

I used carbon tracing paper and traced the sections of the stays onto the workpieces, making sure to draw in the joinery. This eliminates any of the guesswork in application, especially after the pieces are rough shaped. Don't forget to clearly label each section as you go! Next, mark out the tabletop supports. I used a backsaw to cut the straight sides of the round center areas and a bowsaw to make the half-round cuts. Refine the shape with rasps, files, and sandpaper, clamping the two supports together for continuity while shaping.

Join the sections of the stays with bridle joints and wooden dowels for added insurance. It can be challenging to lay out the joinery after the pieces are cut round because the curved sides make referencing a square almost impossible. This is why full-size drawings are so important and the joinery is laid out beforehand. The ends of the stays are tenoned into the supports. After sawing the tenons, mark the mortise locations in the supports.

Once the joinery is complete for the supports and stays, refine the shapes of the curved

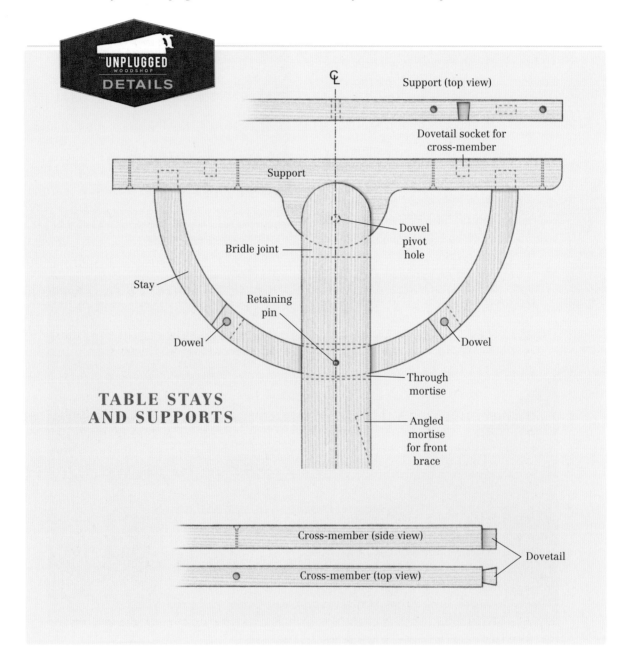

**TABLE STAYS
AND SUPPORTS**

1. Check the pieces with the full-size drawings as reference. 2. Saw the bridle joints in the stays and dry-fit the parts.
3. Before the final shaping, pin the bridle joints with wooden dowels. 4. Scribe the mortises in the supports.

components with rasps, files, spokeshaves, and finally sandpaper—whatever it takes to fair the curves and make these things round…ish! Trust your eye: The stays don't have to be perfect half-circles.

The tabletop supports pivot on a ½-in. hardwood dowel. The holes for the dowels are drilled from the inside of the legs and stop halfway through the outside wall of the leg-top bridle joints. Mark these locations next and drill them. For the stopped holes in the outside walls of the joint, I used a Forstner® bit instead of an auger bit. The auger bit has a fairly long lead screw and the extra length may punch through

Drill mating holes in the legs and tabletop supports.

to the outside of the leg. The Forstner bit is slower in the brace, but for the sake of two holes, it's just the ticket for this application. Also drill the mating holes through the center round section of the top supports.

Now you're ready to dry-fit the parts. Do this in two stages: First, feed the stays through the through mortises and then insert the top supports down into the bridle joints. Press the tenons into the mating mortises and insert the ½-in. dowels through the holes. You'll need to do a few trial runs. Leave the main tabletop pivot dowels long for now; the extra length will serve as a handle while you work, and you'll be removing them a few more times through the building process.

Once fit, check to make sure the supports actually pivot. If they bottom out inside the joinery, pare the bottom insides of the mortises until the supports and stays pivot freely. Too loose isn't good either. You need to sneak up on a good-fitting joint, which usually means cutting the mortise a little snug and planing the

HOW MANY POSITIONS FOR YOUR TABLETOP?

IN EARLY ARCHITECT'S tables, you'll find location holes every inch or two as the stays are made of metal. Use your own judgment with the number of stops, but keep in mind that the more holes you make, the weaker the stays will become. If you are making a series of stop locations, do the drilling with the base dry-fit and drill through the existing hole on the inside of the legs. Check to see where the retaining pinholes fall on your stays before you commit to drilling them.

Dry-fit the support and stay assembly, leaving the ½-in. dowel and the rod for the retaining pins long for now. The pins will be cut down and knobs attached later in the build.

supports until they just sneak in without too much resistance. I like a bit of resistance because there is nothing sweeter than the sound of wooden joinery moving: the burnished surfaces gliding across one another, the smallest detection of a creak here or there, at least for the first few times. These are the desirable characteristics of hand-crafted, wooden furniture. This is the continued pleasure you get from using it.

Next mark the holes for the retaining pins that hold the tabletop at different angles. Again, the retaining pinholes go through the inside of the legs only, pass through the stays, and stop before exiting the outside wall of the leg. The number of dedicated position stops for the table is up to you (see the sidebar on the facing page). I started with one hole on-center for flat tabletop work, and a second position for sketching or drawing full-scale plans. I may decide to add more later, but I suspect I'll be using the table either flat as a desktop or angled for drawing.

I used ¼-in. brass rod for the retaining pins, but you could use wooden dowel or any metal rod you have around your shop. (I wouldn't use anything smaller than a ¼-in. or larger than ½-in. dia.) With the components dry-fit, drill the pin stop holes and test-fit the leg assemblies.

BEADING THE LEGS AND REFINING THE FEET

Now that the supports and stays are complete, dismantle the leg assemblies and scratch some beads into the outside of the legs, if desired. (Another decorative option is to add some stringing or maybe some carved details.) If you decide to add a bead, start with the straight sides of the legs and then carefully move onto the round tops. Scratching a bead across grain is tricky business. Take your time and use a light touch.

At this point the feet are still flat along their bottom. For a more stable footprint, remove the bottom middle area of the feet to create four points of contact. Scribe the waste area and then make a series of crosscuts across the

bottom of the feet. The waste can be easily chopped out with a wide chisel.

Refine the front profiles of the feet as well and round over the outside bottom corners. The softened edges, to my eyes at least, make for a sweeter profile. Chamfer the top perimeter of the feet. After shaping the feet and beading the legs, I dry-fit the pieces (of course) to see how things are progressing.

Start the bead on the sides of the legs and then work the profile around the top rounded section. Cross-grain beading can be a bit of a challenge so take your time and use light passes. Use a small detail chisel to refine the bead and sandpaper to blend the curves.

1. To profile the bottom of the feet, make a series of crosscuts across the marked area and remove the waste with a heavy chisel.

2. In no time at all the feet are finished. 3. A chamfer at the top and rounded bottom corners softens the profile of the feet.

CUTTING THE CROSS-STRETCHERS

With the leg assemblies complete, mark and cut the mortise locations for the cross-stretchers. These are straightforward mortise-and-tenon joints. I used one large tenon here, but you might want to err on the side of caution and split this one into a twin tenon for added insurance. Or consider a through tenon for a completely different looking table.

Refer to the cut list on p. 53 and dimension the cross-stretchers. Cut and dry-fit the tenons into the corresponding leg mortises. The two upright pieces in the middle of the stretchers should also be cut and joined at this point.

ADDING THE TABLETOP CROSS-MEMBERS

To increase the rigidity of the tabletop supports I added two cross-members, dovetailing them into the two supports. Adding the cross-members makes the entire assembly move as one unit that is jointed together, which is better than relying on the screws to move the assembly as one. Crosscut the pieces and then saw the shoulders into the ends. Mark and cut the dovetails, lay the pieces in place across the supports, and scribe the dovetails. This process is the same as cutting any half-blind dovetail socket; the sides are sawn at a 45° angle and then the waste is removed with a chisel. After another dry-fit, predrill the supports as well as these two cross-members using a drill bit that is larger than the screws you'll use to attach the top.

You don't have to worry too much about wood movement in the long cross-members because they're running in the same direction as the tabletop, but the tabletop supports need to be addressed. I'm making the tabletop from laminated maple so wood movement will be minimal. The large screw holes will give enough wiggle room for the small amount of movement expected. If you use flatsawn stock for the top, these holes should be elongated to allow for seasonal wood movement.

Predrill the tabletop supports with oversize holes to allow for a bit of wood movement.

You could make the tabletop out of full-width, flatsawn planks; if you do, make sure to elongate the screw holes in the supports to allow for wood movement.

TIP

1. Cut the dovetails on the ends of the cross-members and mark the socket locations in the top supports. 2. Round the edges on the tabletop cross-members and dry-fit the parts.

MAKING THE TABLETOP

I used 5/4 curly maple for the top. The beauty of the maple is amplified through the edge grain. The curl is much more pronounced in the edge, so I decided it would be worth my while to rip the maple planks into 1½-in. strips and then laminate them all back together on edge, which will not only highlight the figure in the wood but also make for a much more stable top. Wood generally moves the most across the grain so by using it on edge, the expansion and contraction will be kept to a minimum.

That said, take your best ripsaw and start sawing. You might be thinking the 24-plus ripping cuts in the 3-ft., 5/4 maple are a lot of extra work ... and you'd be right! But the results in the finished piece will be well worth

After some time with a ripsaw and handplane, the 24 curly maple strips for the tabletop are ready for glue-up.

Building the tabletop in two sections makes it easier to flatten the whole.

the effort. Eat your oatmeal and put on a fresh pot of coffee.

After ripping the stock, glue up the top in two sections to make the process a little more manageable. Dealing with curly maple like this means using a high-angle plane to control tearout. And using a high-angle plane involves muscle power, so flattening and smoothing the tops in two 12-in. widths will be easier than working on one full piece. Trust me on this one.

THE BREADBOARD ENDS

With the two top pieces flattened and smooth, you can joint and glue the two halves to create

1. Dry-fit the breadboard ends and mark the tenon locations for drilling. 2. Drill the dowel holes through the tenons. I used Miller dowels and a dedicated bit; usually associated with power tools, the bit works fine in my old brace. 3. Detail showing breadboard end mortises and drilled tenons. 4. Elongate the dowel holes on the two outside tenons.

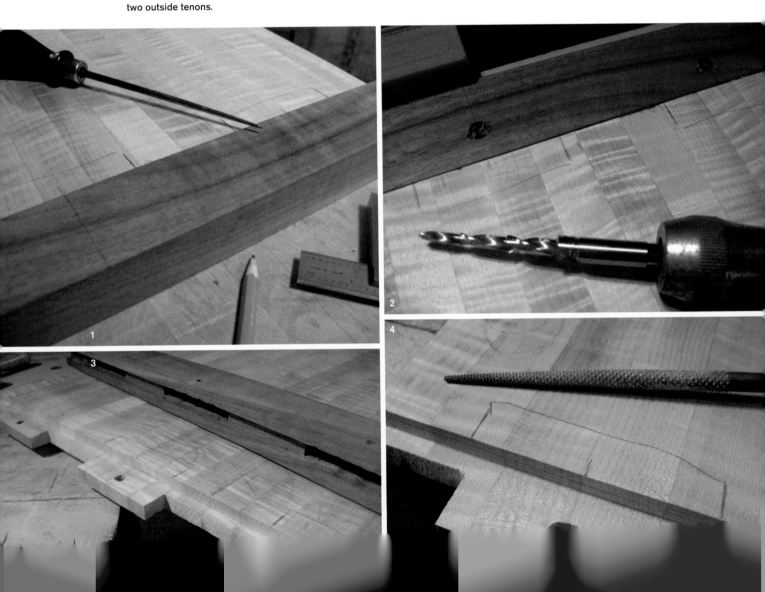

1. Glue the breadboard ends to the tabletop. 2. Trim the dowels with a flush-cutting saw. 3. Plane the breadboards and dowels flush with the tabletop. Use a high-angle smoothing plane and a card scraper for the final smoothing.

the full tabletop. Once the glue sets, dress the middle joint and crosscut the ends square. Clean up the sawmarks and lay out the tenons for the breadboard ends. The ends add a decorative element but will also keep the tabletop flat through the years.

Make deep scribe lines across the width of the tabletop and mark the thickness of the tenons. Use a skew rabbet or moving Fillister plane to remove the bulk of the waste and a shoulder plane to refine the tenon cheeks. At this stage you'll have one long tenon across the ends of the tabletop. Divide this up into four separate tenons, leaving a ½-in. tongue between them. Establish the width of the tenons with a series of ripcuts and remove the waste with a fretsaw or bowsaw.

After the tenons are complete, it's time to dimension the stock for the breadboard ends. Leave the breadboards a little thicker than the finished tabletop; the extra thickness will be planed flush after the glue-up. I was originally planning on using maple but ran short on my supply, so I decided to use the same walnut I used for the base. The contrasting woods work well in this design.

Scribe the breadboard and cut the matching groove along its length. I used a plow plane for this step. Dry-fit the breadboard on the table-

top and mark the tenon locations. Make the two outside mortises about ½-in. longer than needed to allow for any wood movement. (This step is crucial if you're using flatsawn stock for the top.) Bore out the waste with an auger bit and refine the mortises with a chisel. Use a router plane to fine-tune the fit.

Dry-fit the breadboard again and mark the locations of the tenons. Drill down through

> When you crosscut the breadboard stock to length, leave it long for now; the "horns" on the ends will make it easier to dry-fit the pieces and disassemble them as you work. They'll also prevent any blowout in the end grain while you cut the mortises.

TIP

the center of the assembled joints so you can insert wooden dowels after the assembly is glued. Once drilled, remove the breadboard and elongate the two outside tenon holes using a round file. When you glue the breadboards in place, apply glue to the center tenons only. Use glue on the dowels as well. The elongated tenons and the holes for the dowels will let the top expand and contract through the seasons without splitting the wood.

With the joinery complete, crosscut the breadboards to their finished length and glue them to the tabletop. As mentioned, apply glue to the two middle tenons only. Glue the dowels and hammer them down through the joints. When the glue is set, trim the dowels with a flush-cutting saw and plane the breadboards flush.

After the top is smooth, turn the piece over and dress the bottom. The next step is to chamfer the tabletop edges. You may decide to add an alternate edge profile such as a

THOUGHTS ON FINISHING

AS YOU READ through the projects in this book, you'll notice that I try to prefinish my work before assembly. It's much easier to apply a finish to the separate components before the final glue-up. For this piece, I'm using dewaxed, super-blond shellac. I apply three coats before the assembly, sanding lightly between each coat. I didn't apply any oil/varnish before the shellac because I find with walnut that I get the most pleasant color with this application. The shellac makes the curl in this maple shine like a wild Atlantic salmon.

Pencil chamfers on both the top and bottom of the tabletop and plane down to the pencil lines.

bullnose, bevel, or even a bead down the edge. If you ever plan on attaching a straightedge, paper holder, or square (see photo 3 on p. 73), you may want to keep it simple and relatively square. I'm going to make a movable straightedge that will serve as a paper tray, a ruler and phone dock (just kidding...at least about the phone dock!). Use your imagination and see what you come up with. Once complete, the table is ready for prefinishing.

GLUING UP THE TABLE

Now the table base is ready for the final glue-up. I use hot hide glue and start with the leg assemblies. Do a dry-run to see how the pieces fit together. For example, the shorter braces need to be inserted into the legs before the two are lowered into the foot mortises. Then, just before the two are driven home, the longer angled brace is inserted. After the two leg assemblies are glued, the cross-stretchers are added and the entire assembly is clamped.

For stress-free assemblies, always do a practice run.

STAYS, SUPPORTS, AND THEN ONTO THE TOP

After the glue is set and the clamps are removed, brush some shellac into the through mortises where the stays pass through and a little into the top bridle joint. You'll be able to see into these cavities when the tabletop is angled, but a couple of light coats of shellac are all that's required. The devil is in the details!

The table supports and stays are next, and the glue-up goes something like this: Insert the stays through the open mortises and apply glue to the tenons. Press the table supports down into the leg-top bridle joints and draw the tenons down into the mortises. Insert the ½-in. pivot dowels to position the pieces. I added

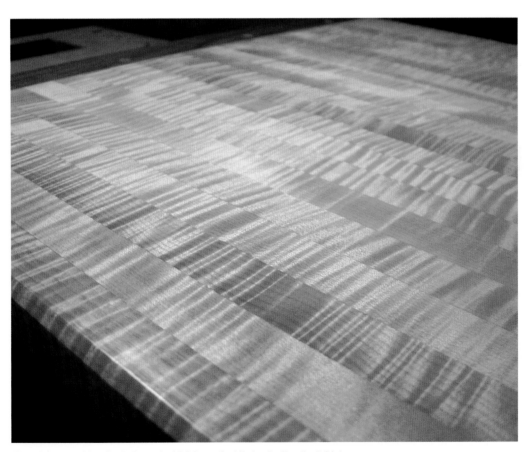

This photo should make it clear why I felt it worthwhile laminating the tabletop.

Attach the tabletop to the stay and support assembly.

screws down through the top supports and into the tenons to bring the stays up tight. This works better than trying to jig up a method for clamping these curved components together.

When the glue is set in the supports and stays, trim the ½-in. maple dowels that are inserted through the leg tops with a flush-cutting saw.

I didn't use any glue on these but pressure-fit only. If you do need to use glue, make sure not to get any of it on the moving parts.

Also trim the brass rods for the pin stops and make up small knobs for the ends. You could turn your own, but if you don't have a lathe you could easily make some rounded knobs using the same method used for the hubs for the Lying Press (see p. 81). You could also leave the knobs square or find a store-bought piece of hardware to suit this application. Maybe old handplane knobs would work? I think I'll try that, just for fun.

With the stays and support details complete, place the tabletop face down on your bench (cover the top with a heavy blanket to protect the finish), center the base, and screw it in place. I gave the entire piece a once-over with super-fine steel wool and some citrus wax for a final finish that is renewable and as smooth as silk.

A vintage handplane knob is reclaimed for the pin stop handles.

"Try to learn something about everything and everything about something."

—Thomas H. Huxley

LYING PRESS

ONE FINE DAY a little more than a decade ago, I was visiting a traditional bookbinder's studio and noticed a beautiful wooden vise with twin hardwood screws and leather-lined jaws. It looked like the ideal solution to holding work in my own woodshop. I eventually came to know this workshop appliance as a *lying* or *finishing* press, and bookmakers have been using it in the art of book crafting for centuries.

Ideal when fastened to a heavy stand-alone frame but just as effective when fixed to a benchtop or make-shift worktable, the lying press is perfect for securing wide panels for any kind of edge work application and excels for drawer making and sawing dovetails. With a couple of blocks of hardwood and some large screws you can buy or build, you'll have a work-holding jig that is second to none.

Recently, commercial hardware has been made available for this style press (see "Commercial Hardware Options" on p. 78), which has been nicknamed a *Moxon* vise, after Joseph Moxon (1627–1691), an English printer of mathematical books and maps. Moxon wrote *The Art of Joinery*, one of the earliest texts available on woodworking, as well as *Mechanick Exercises: Or, The Doctrine of Handy-works*, which explores the arts of smithing, joinery, carpentry, turning, and "bricklayery." Other examples of similar twin-screw vises are also found in early texts by André Jacob Roubo and André Félibien.

SELECTING MATERIALS

The first things to consider for this project are the screws. You can make them (as explained here) or use an aftermarket variety either made of wood or metal. As you'll see, if you decide to make them, you'll need a special-purpose wood-threading tool and some straight-grained 1½-in. dowel stock. The wood-threading kits are available through special-order tool dealers. I purchased mine at Woodcraft® (www.woodcraft.com).

Besides the screws there really isn't too much material needed. I purchased a few large planks of walnut for some of the furniture projects that appear later in the book, and inevitably when you buy roughsawn

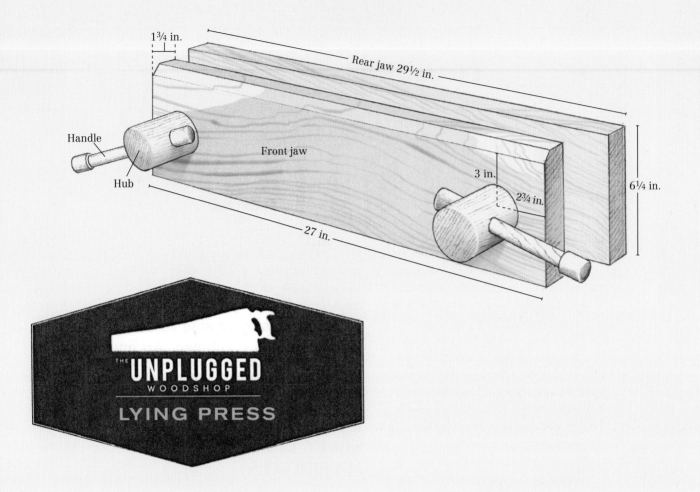

1¾ in.

Rear jaw 29½ in.

Handle

Hub

Front jaw

3 in.

2¾ in.

6¼ in.

27 in.

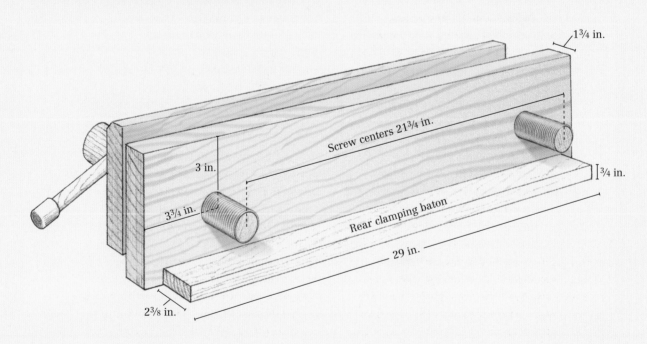

1¾ in.

Screw centers 21¾ in.

3 in.

¾ in.

3¾ in.

Rear clamping baton

2⅜ in.

29 in.

THE UNPLUGGED WOODSHOP
LYING PRESS

The press is attached to the benchtop with holdfasts.

lumber there will be undesirable areas with knots, checks, and other blemishes that make it unsuitable for fine furniture construction. This walnut was no exception, and at the end of one of the planks were a couple of knots with some reversing grain and large areas of sapwood. I decided to use this stock for the jaws and rear clamping baton on my press. I'm not overly concerned with the aesthetics of the wood but more with the size and weight. The walnut plank I had was just over 2 in. thick and around 13 in. wide.

PREPARING THE STOCK

To begin, crosscut and rip the stock to the desired dimension. (You'll notice that the ripping notch on the new saw bench is already coming in handy!) With the two jaws roughed out, dimension them to their finished sizes at the workbench. You'll see from the drawing that the front jaw on my press, at 27 in., is slightly shorter than the rear, which finishes at 29½ in. This difference in length creates "shoulders" on

C U T · L I S T		
FRONT JAW	1	1¾ IN. × 6¼ IN. × 27 IN.
REAR JAW	1	1¾ IN. × 6¼ IN. × 29½ IN.
REAR CLAMPING BATON	1	¾ IN. × 2⅜ IN. × 29 IN.
DOWEL FOR WOODEN SCREWS	2	1½ IN. DIA. × 13½ IN.
HUBS	2	2½ IN. DIA. × 3½ IN.
DOWEL FOR HANDLES	2	¾ IN. DIA. × 8 IN.
HANDLE END CAPS	4	1 IN. SQ.

the rear jaw that are convenient when clamps are required to hold the press while in use.

BORING THE HOLES

With the two jaws flat, square, and dimensioned to final size, the next step is to bore the holes for the hand screws. Boring a 1½-in. hole by hand through what is now 1¾-in. walnut isn't as easy as you may think. Physically, it isn't difficult, but finding a suitable auger bit

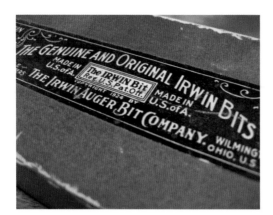

My vintage Irwin expansion bits get a good workout during this project.

COMMERCIAL HARDWARE OPTIONS

THERE ARE A FEW different configurations of commercial hardware for the lying press, or Moxon vise, currently offered. In one popular example (available from Bench Crafted, www.benchcrafted. com), metal screws are captured in the rear jaw and protrude out through the front. Cast-iron handwheels attach to the screws at the front of the vise and provide the clamping pressure needed. The screws don't turn in this design, only the handwheels do.

Another configuration that is similar to the lying press I've modeled this project after has metal screws traveling in from the front and threading into captured bolts mounted in the rear (available from Tools For Working Wood, www.toolsforworkingwood.com). Both of these examples use metal hardware and may be a suitable alternative for anyone not wanting to make his or her own wooden screws.

that size certainly is. I'm lucky enough to have a set of vintage expansion bits that were manufactured by the Irwin® Auger Bit Company in the mid-1950s. You may have success using a modern spade bit if you don't have anything this size already in your kit.

Refer to "Lying Press" drawing on p. 76 and carefully lay out the locations of the holes. The front jaw receives 1½-in. holes so the dowels can pass through, while the rear jaw holes need to be 1⅜ in. to thread. If you're using commercial hardware, refer to "Commercial Hardware Options" at right and lay out the hardware locations accordingly.

Bore the two 1½-in. holes in the front jaw, and then use a rasp and slightly elongate the

1. A white pencil line is easier to see when working with dark woods. 2. Rip-cut the stock to dimension.

holes to create oval shapes. Make these holes only about ⅛ in. larger on their horizontal axis; the screws should still fit snug from top to bottom. The elongated holes will provide enough of an angle so that when a workpiece is clamped in the press and you want to re-

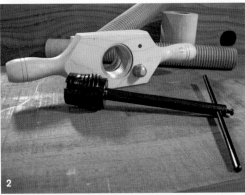

1. An expansion bit is the tool to use for boring the 1½-in. holes in the front jaw. 2. Wood-threading kits are readily available through specialty tool dealers. 3. Tap the 1⅜-in. holes in the rear jaw.

adjust it, you'll have to loosen only one side of the press to do so. The oval holes allow the front jaw to rack a little, which in this case is a good thing.

Continue by measuring and marking the locations for the holes in the rear jaw. These rear jaw holes *do not* get elongated. They'll be tapped for the screws to thread into and should be 1⅜ in. dia.

TAPPING THE HOLES IN THE REAR JAW

The wood-threading kit I use for making 1½-in. screws requires a 1⅜-in. hole to receive the tap. I use a liberal amount of boiled linseed oil and make sure everything is well lubricated before attempting to tap the holes. Begin the tap as straight as you can and slowly proceed until you're completely through to the back side of the jaw.

I've read many reviews from woodworkers who have had less than ideal results when using wood-threading kits. Most blame the kit and say it's due to poor manufacturing, but it's my experience that the dowels used for the screws are usually the problem. Make sure you're using straight-grained hardwood that is perfectly round. For this reason, I don't recommend you turn your own dowels unless you're a very accomplished wood turner. Nor do I recommend you purchase dowel stock from big-box-style hardware stores. These are often oval in cross section, and you'll get poor results when trying to thread them.

Source out a reliable wood mill or dealer and buy high-grade, well-seasoned stock. The dowel I used for this project is hard maple and

The cut list for this project is shown on p. 77, but bear in mind that the measurements given aren't critical to make a lying press; use whatever stock you have. The jaw heights should be the same as one another but the rest is completely subjective. Read through the entire chapter before assembling the cut list; a good practice for all of the projects.

TIP

Clamp the dowel in a shoulder vise and cut threads to within 2 in. of the end.

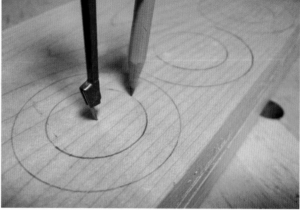

Lay out four circles that will make up the hub blanks.

has beautiful straight grain. It's perfectly round and has been carefully dried and stored. The night before I plan on threading the screws I'll take my two dowels, which are crosscut to 13½ in. in length, and soak them overnight in boiled linseed oil. These small steps should be carefully followed for successful wood threading.

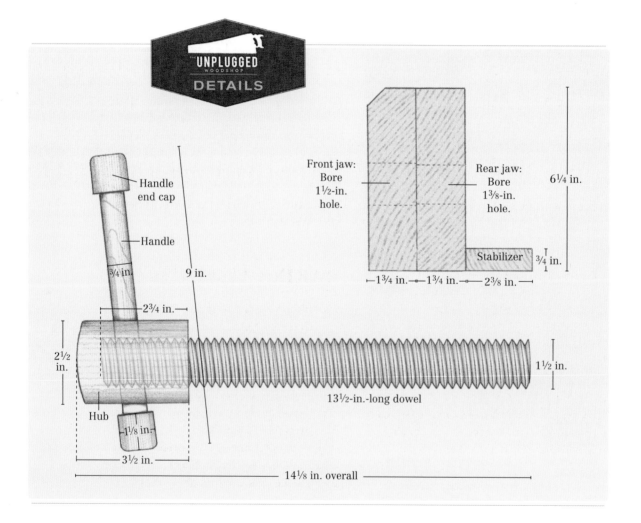

UNPLUGGED
WOODSHOP
DETAILS

Handle end cap

Handle

Handle

¾ in.

9 in.

2¾ in.

2½ in.

Hub

1⅛ in.

3½ in.

13½-in.-long dowel

1½ in.

14⅛ in. overall

Front jaw:
Bore
1½-in.
hole.

Rear jaw:
Bore
1⅜-in.
hole.

6¼ in.

Stabilizer

¾ in.

1¾ in. — 1¾ in. — 2⅜ in.

1. Glue up the hub blanks. 2. Plane the four corners down to the pencil lines. 3. Four sides planed to 8 and then to 16. 4. The finished hub is far from a perfect circle but it's suitable for this application.

Clamp the oil-saturated dowels in your shoulder vise using a square to ensure they're absolutely straight. Slowly and carefully begin threading, applying light but constant and steady pressure. Work your way down, adjusting the dowel height as needed. Leave the last 2 in. of dowel unthreaded; it will get glued into a hub later in the process. Complete this same process with the second dowel, again leaving about 2 in. of space at the end. This area will receive a hub in the next step.

MAKING THE HUBS

The hubs prevent the screws from passing through the front jaw holes while providing an area for the handles to attach. The hub shoulders also provide the clamping force needed for the press to function properly.

To begin, prepare some stock that's 1¾ in. thick (I used hard maple again). Using a compass, draw four 1½-in. circles, with a second circle around the first at 2½ in. using the same center locations to reference the pin of the compass (see the right photo on the facing page).

With the hubs laid out, bore out the middle using a 1½-in. bit. Bore two of the holes completely through the stock and the last two only halfway through the material. Saw out the blanks. You should have two blanks with holes that go all the way through and two with holes that stop about halfway through the thickness of the stock. Take one of the blanks with the hole all the way through and glue it to one that has the stopped hole bored in it. Do the same with the other two blanks.

Once the glue has set, get ready for a fun exercise in handplaning. Clamp the blank in a vise and plane down to create an octagon. Essentially, we're knocking off the four corners to begin. (You could save some time and saw off the outside corners to start with, but where's the fun in that?) With the four corners planed away, repeat this step and make the 8-sided blank into one with 16 sides. Continue this process until you have a rough cylindrical shape. It doesn't have to be perfect—we're not reinventing the wheel here! Plane the face and the end and remove any tearout that may have occurred while rounding. A small chamfer or roundover at the front is also a nice touch. Follow this same procedure for the second hub blank.

With the two hubs roughed out, you can refine the shape with a file and sandpaper or leave them a little rough. To be honest, they could be left square if you'd prefer: It's really just an aesthetic choice to round them over and it doesn't affect their function. When complete, glue the hubs to the ends of the screws.

BORING THE HUBS

When the glue is dry, bore the ¾-in. holes through the hubs and insert ¾-in. wooden dowels for turn handles. If the handles pass straight through the hubs, it doesn't leave much room for gripping so I angled the holes in the hubs a little, resulting in handles that protrude on slight angles out from the front jaw. The slight angle (about 2° off of 90°) saves your knuckles while in use and makes turning the screws a bit easier. Again, small details can really make a difference in use.

The length of the handle is up to you, but begin with something in the 8-in. to 10-in. range. I made mine 8 in. long, and when the end cap is applied they finish at 9 in. Experiment to find something that feels good for you.

Glue the hubs to the ends of the screws and set aside to dry.

1. Bore ¾-in. holes in the hubs. (Photo by Nelson Fidgen, age 7.) 2. Boring the hub holes at a slight angle (about 2° off of 90°) keeps the handles away from the jaw while in use. 3. The finished hubs.

THE REAR CLAMPNG BATON

The final piece of the main press assembly is a rear clamping baton or stabilizer. This is made from ¾-in. stock, 2⅜ in. wide, and about the same length as the rear jaw. I had a scrap left over that was about an inch shy of the rear jaw length but it works just as well. Prep the piece

as per usual and glue it to the lower back of the rear jaw. This clamping baton is essential when using holdfasts to secure the press to your benchtop. When the glue is dry, clean up the bottom of the joint with a sharp handplane.

With the rear jaw and clamping baton complete, I next plane a wide chamfer in the top outside edge of the front jaw (see "Chamfer the Front Jaw" on p. 84).

CHAMFER THE FRONT JAW

A CHAMFER IN THE outside edge of the front jaw comes in handy when sawing half-blind dovetails and you have to hold a saw at a 45° angle to your workpiece. Lay out some guide lines about ½ in. in and down from the top front corner and plane the profile into the top edge as shown.

1. Lay out lines for a chamfer in the front jaw.
2. Plane down to the pencil lines.

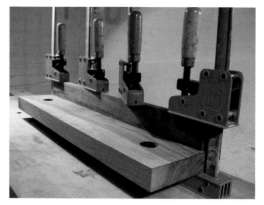

Glue the clamping baton to the back lower edge of the rear jaw.

HANDLE END CAPS

One last handle detail to finish off before final assembly is to make the end caps. This is pretty much the same process we followed when making the hubs earlier but on a smaller scale (see p. 81). Using 1-in. stock and a compass, draw some ¾-in. circles with a second 1-in. circle around them. Bore ¾-in. holes about halfway through the stock and cut out the caps. With a plane, file, and sandpaper, round the caps over until they're a comfortable shape. The caps will be glued to the ends of the handles after final assembly.

FINAL ASSEMBLY AND DETAILS

With the press components complete, give all of the surfaces a good rub of oil/varnish to finish and protect them. If you have some scraps of leather left over from other projects, you could use some here to line the jaws. It's a nice touch but it isn't essential.

To assemble the press, stand the jaws on your benchtop and insert the screws through the front holes and begin threading them into the rear jaw. Insert the ¾-in. dowels for the handles and tighten. Glue the end caps onto the handles. When dry, clamp the press in place using either holdfasts on the rear clamping baton (my preference) or front clamps attached to the shoulders of the rear jaw.

You're now ready to go to work with your new lying press. Enjoy!

THE POCHADE BOX

"Drawing is the artist's most direct and spontaneous expression."

—Edgar Degas

POCHADE BOX

SIDE VIEW

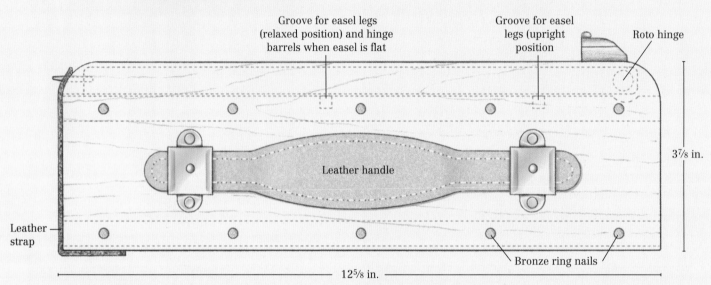

Groove for easel legs (relaxed position) and hinge barrels when easel is flat

Groove for easel legs (upright position)

Roto hinge

Leather handle

3⅞ in.

Leather strap

Bronze ring nails

12⅝ in.

FRONT VIEW

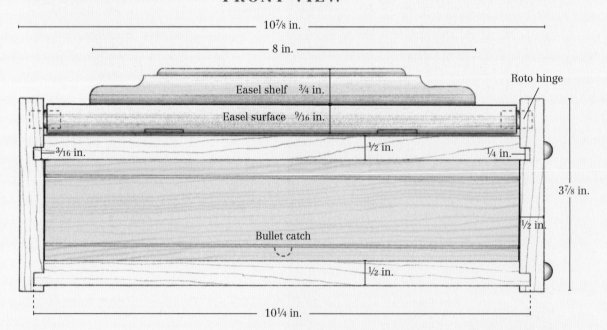

10⅞ in.

8 in.

Easel shelf   ¾ in.

Easel surface   ⁹⁄₁₆ in.

Roto hinge

³⁄₁₆ in.

½ in.

¼ in.

3⅞ in.

Bullet catch

½ in.

½ in.

10¼ in.

THE TERM *POCHADE* comes from the French verb *pocher*, which means "to sketch"; the word *poche* is French for "pocket." So perhaps the pochade box lies somewhere between the two? A pocket to hold a sketch? That works for me.

Pochade boxes became popular with French painters through the eighteenth and nineteenth centuries. The pochade box was a relatively small, portable wooden tote an artist could transport outdoors. A hinged lid opens and acts as a makeshift easel, while the interior holds the art supplies. This way, the artists could quickly capture an image, idea, or a scene and then later expand or re-create it in a larger format back inside a studio setting. This notion

C U T · L I S T

DRAWER SIDES	2	$7/16$ IN. × 2 IN. × 12 IN.
DRAWER FRONT AND BACK	2	$11/16$ IN. × 2 IN. × $9\,7/8$ IN.
DRAWER BOTTOM (MADE FROM TWO PARTS)	1	$5/16$ IN. × $9\,1/4$ IN. × $11\,3/4$ IN.
PENCIL TRAY SUPPORTS	2	$1/8$ IN. × 1 IN. × $11\,1/4$ IN.
PENCIL TRAY (FITS INSIDE DRAWER BOX)	1	$1/2$ IN. × 6 IN. × $8\,15/16$ IN.
CARCASE SIDES	2	$1/2$ IN. × $3\,7/8$ IN. × $12\,5/8$ IN.
TOP AND BOTTOM PANELS	2	$1/2$ IN. × $10\,1/4$ IN. × $12\,5/8$ IN.
EASEL (MADE FROM STRIPS OF OFFCUTS)	1	$9/16$ IN. × $9\,3/4$ IN. × $12\,3/8$ IN.
EASEL SUPPORT ARMS	2	$1/8$ IN. × $7/8$ IN. × $6\,5/8$ IN.
EASEL SHELF (SHAPED TO PLAN)	1	$3/4$ IN. × $3/4$ IN. × 8 IN.

One of the more famous depictions of a pochade box is Vincent van Gogh's *On the Road to Tarascon*, painted in 1888. Sadly, this work no longer exists as it is said to have been burned during World War II when allied forces bombed Magdeburg, Germany.

DRAWER (SIDE VIEW)

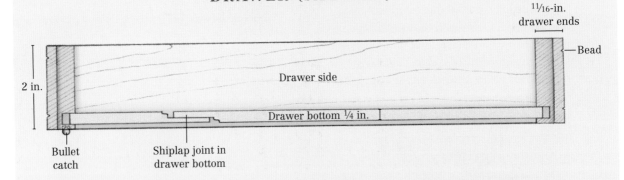

1¹⁄₁₆-in.
drawer ends

Bead

2 in.

Drawer side

Drawer bottom ¼ in.

Bullet
catch

Shiplap joint in
drawer bottom

DRAWER (TOP VIEW)

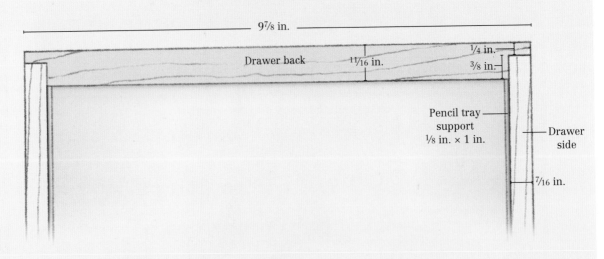

9⁷⁄₈ in.

Drawer back

1¹⁄₁₆ in.

¼ in.

³⁄₈ in.

Pencil tray
support
¹⁄₈ in. × 1 in.

Drawer
side

⁷⁄₁₆ in.

of quickly capturing ideas appeals to me, and I keep this box at arm's length near my workbench for whenever inspiration strikes me.

The design shown here is my own interpretation of a pochade box. I use it for sketching ideas with pencil and paper so I can then expand on them later either in a computer program like SketchUp or by means of full-scale drawings or mockups. I'm inspired by the pochade box with all its romanticism and designed this benchtop easel and storage container so I'll always have my pencils and sketchbook handy. The pochade box is a great introduction to basic box building using simple rabbet joints and ring nails. It's also a fun little project to fill in a weekend of shop time.

QUICK-AND-EASY DRAWER CONSTRUCTION

Nine times out of ten, when building furniture with drawers, the carcase is made first and the drawers are carefully fit into the openings. For this project, I decided to do things in reverse. Why? Because this design is an open-ended box with a drawer that's accessible from both ends. Fitting a double-ended drawer into a carcase can be a challenge, so I decided it would be much easier to build the drawer first and then fit the box around it.

A drawer with nailed rabbet joints is quick and easy to build and still plenty strong enough for this application. If you'd like to make your drawer a little fancier, some half-blind dovetails may be the ticket (see p. 181). I'm using a simplified method for this project, but don't worry, there'll be plenty of drawer making in later projects so you'll get lots of dovetailing practice!

In traditional drawer making, when using solid wood for the drawer bottom, the drawer back is made narrower than the sides and front. The drawer bottom is fit in grooves cut underneath the drawer back to allow for wood movement through seasonal humidity changes. In this case, we have a double-ended drawer with a full front and back that uses solid wood throughout. This may seem like a recipe for disaster, but we'll get around the wood movement issues by giving the drawer bottom some room to grow. You'll see what I mean as we get into the build.

To get started, select your drawer stock and dimension it according to the cut list. To keep the pieces in the proper order, mark the edges with building triangles, as shown in photo 2 below these make it easy to orientate the components as you work through the project.

CUTTING THE RABBET JOINTS

Scribe the rabbet joints on the front and back of the drawer with a marking gauge, using the width of the drawer side as reference for the width of the joint. Mark the shoulders of the rabbet joint on the inside ends of the drawer front and back. The depth of the joint is cut to ⅜ in. Using a bench hook and backsaw,

1. Drawer parts dimensioned and ready for some simple joinery. 2. Building triangles keep pieces in order.

1. Set the marking gauge using the drawer side as reference—no rulers required! 2. Scribe the lines on the inside of the drawer ends. 3. Crosscut the shoulders. 4. Rip-cut the cheek and, as always, fine-tune the joinery with a sharp chisel and check it for square.

crosscut the shoulders. With the shoulder cuts complete, clamp the piece in your face vise and rip-cut the cheek to finish the joint.

Fine-tune the fit with a paring chisel and check all of your joinery. Dry-fit the sides to the drawer front and back and make sure everything is square. Attention to detail now will pay

off later when you build the carcase around the drawer. If the drawer isn't square, you'll never have a good fit later.

FITTING THE DRAWER BOTTOM

Using a small plow plane, the next step is to cut a ¼-in.-wide groove, ⅛ in. up from the bottom of the drawer sides. My plane has a depth stop set for ³⁄₁₆ in. deep; when the plane stops taking shavings, I know I'm done. The front and back of the drawer also receive a groove, but I make these ¹⁄₂ in. deep. The extra depth will allow space for the drawer bottom to expand.

After the grooves are cut in the drawer sides and ends, measure and prepare the stock for the bottom. I'm using two oversize pieces of ⁵⁄₁₆-in.-thick poplar. The extra thickness will add some strength to the drawer and will hold up through many years of use. Mill the stock to width but keep some extra length for now. A shiplap joint cut into the drawer bottom panels will allow room for wood movement (this is the "room to grow" I mentioned in the introduction). Begin by planing a rabbet along the bottom edges so the bottom pieces fit snugly into the ¹⁄₄-in. drawer bottom groove. I do this with my rabbet plane set for a fine cut.

The rabbet plane is also used to cut the 1-in. overlap on the shiplap joint where the two parts of the drawer bottom meet. This joint along with the deep grooves in the drawer front and back will allow plenty of room for the bottom to expand when the humidity changes. When

PENCIL IN THE WASTE

It's a good idea to pencil in the waste area on all of your joinery. This is a good habit to get into even on a straightforward lap joint. A minute now may save hours later if you were to accidentally saw on the wrong side of the lines.

A plow plane makes quick work of the grooves for a drawer bottom. The fence and depth stop ensure accurate results.

The drawer bottom is made from two panels with a shiplap joint to allow wood movement. The bottom panels are free to move when they expand.

WORKING WITH WAXED LINE

TIP

A few years ago, my father-in-law gave me a spool of waxed line. He said it was used by butchers to wrap meat as well as by mail carriers to tie heavy loads. If you can get your hands on some, it's great for holding components for dry-fits as well as for many other workshop applications. I used it here in a Spanish windlass knot to keep the drawer together for a dry-fit. Check a leather supplier and ask for waxed linen thread (it's sometimes called 6/4 cord in upholstery shops).

the drawer bottom panels are complete, do a dry-fit to see how much room they'll have for expansion.

BUILDING THE PENCIL TRAY AND SUPPORTS

With a dry-fit complete, measure and check the drawer for square. Next, prepare some stock $1/8$ in. thick that will act as the tray supports. Cut the stock to 1 in. in width and to fit inside the drawer's length (about $11\frac{1}{4}$ in. long). The tray supports will be glued to the inside of the drawer sides during final assembly, so make sure the grain direction is running the same as the drawer sides (see the bottom photo on p. 96).

Now it's time to make the pencil tray. For mine, I used some $1/2$-in. poplar sawn to 9 in. long and 6 in. wide. A rabbet cut in the underside of the tray will rest on the $1/8$-in. supports inside the drawer sides. Using a No. 4, $1/4$-in. molding plane, cut a series of grooves across the width of the tray to hold pencils and other drawing utensils. To begin, make a fence approximately the same size as your molding plane to guide it along the outer edge of the stock. Once the first groove is complete, the

1. A makeshift fence guides the molding plane to begin the grooves. 2. The fence rides in each groove as you work across the tray. 3. Halfway there . . . 4. Once all the grooves are cut, dry-fit the drawer with the pencil tray.

makeshift fence will ride in each groove as you work your way across the tray. It would be difficult to plane a series of straight grooves without some sort of fence, and this method is quick and easy with reliable results.

DRAWER ASSEMBLY AND BEADING

With the drawer components complete, get set for the glue-up. To eliminate any sharp corners on these parts that will be handled so often,

break all of the inside edges and round over the corners of the pencil tray.

When the glue dries on the drawer box, scratch some decorative beads in the tops and bottoms of the drawer front and back. Mine are dictated by the width of the cutter in my beading tool and are about ¼ in. wide. This is a great time to use the lying press to hold the drawer secure. When the carcase is complete and you're satisfied with the fit, drive some ring nails through the rabbet joints to make sure the drawer will stay put.

After the drawer front and back are planed smooth, scratch some beads into them. The lying press is the perfect appliance for working on drawers.

MAKING THE CARCASE

The drawer is now complete (except for the ring nails and a bullet catch that will be added later), so it's time to prep the stock for the carcase. I used ½-in. curly maple and jointed two pieces together to make up the panels for the top and bottom. They should finish at

Apply the ring nails after the final dry-fit is complete inside the main pochade box carcase. This is in case you need to plane a bit of material off the drawer sides to fine-tune the fit later.

TIP

12⅝ in. long by 10¼ in. wide by ½ in. thick. Note that the grain is running side to side to allow for wood movement. The carcase sides are also dimensioned at this time and finish at 12⅝ in. long by 3⅞ in. wide by ½ in. thick.

When the glue is dry, square up and smooth the panels and then lay out and scribe the ¼-in. rabbet joints on the sides. Remove the bulk of the material with a rabbet plane and then use a shoulder plane to refine the joints. Next, cut the grooves into the carcase sides for the top and bottom panels. The top of the lower groove is ⅜ in. up from the bottom, and the top of the upper groove is 2⅞ in. up. Cut these grooves with a small plow plane and then dry-fit. Straightforward joinery is plenty strong enough for this application; some glue and ring nails will hold the box together for many years of use.

Glue the interior pencil tray supports.

Cut the grooves in the carcase sides with a plow plane.

With the joinery cut, dry-fit the carcase.

MAKING THE EASEL

The easel is made from a mosaic of offcuts, which provides a great opportunity to use those special little pieces you've been hoarding for so long! I ripped some random strips and planed them square. They're crosscut to length at 9¾ in. wide, jointed, and glued.

When the glue has dried, plane the easel surface flat and square it to the carcase. I rounded over the ends where the Roto hinges (see p. 37) will be installed to allow the easel to raise and lower. Follow with another dry-fit.

EASEL DETAILS

The easel raises up from the flat position and stands on two small legs that hinge in the back. The main surface hinges on two Roto hinges installed in the sides of one end and mated with corresponding holes drilled in the carcase sides. A Forstner bit in my brace makes quick work of the holes, and I test-fit the piece using wooden dowels made slightly undersize for ease of removal. Plane a round groove in the top of the carcase using a No. 12, ¾-in. molding plane. The groove needs to be only about ³⁄₁₆ in. deep to allow the space required for the rotating end of the easel when raised.

The hinged legs that hold the easel surface in the upright position require somewhere to nest when the easel surface is flat, so I cut out two channels in the bottom of the easel surface for the legs to fit in when not in use. Establish the

perimeter of the cavities with deep scribe lines. Refine the depth with a sharp chisel and mallet followed by a router plane; once the waste is removed, you're ready to fit the legs and attach two small brass hinges. Drill pilot holes for the hinges and use a file to remove the extra length of the screws if necessary.

1. The ripping notch in the sawyer's bench comes in handy while sawing the thin stock for the easel surface. Having thin stock supported on both sides of the kerf while sawing makes the process easier. **2.** Glue a mosaic of offcuts for the easel.

1. Chisel out two stopped dados to give the legs somewhere to go while the surface is not in use. 2. The router plane establishes a consistent depth. 3. Fit the legs into the dadoes and attach the hinges. 4. Test the hinged legs and easel surface with Roto hinges.

Once I've attached the legs and raised the easel surface to where I like it for sketching, I mark the location of the legs and disassemble the carcase. Cut a groove in the carcase top to hold the legs in place while in use and make two more small cavities for the barrel of the hinges to fit in when the easel is flat. Cut the groove with a plow plane and simply chisel out the hinge recesses. After another dry-fit, disassemble the box, round over the top corners of the carcase, and smooth all of the surfaces.

The final stage before finish and assembly is to glue a small shelf to the lower portion of the easel surface. This is where my sketchbook will stand while in use. You can use whatever design you like for this shelf: I grabbed a small piece of walnut from the offcut pile and shaped it with saw, plow plane, and file to give the shelf a bit of an Arts and Crafts feel, which suits me just fine. With the easel shelf attached, give everything a coat of oil/varnish, which is easier to do now before the carcase is glued.

The carcase side removed reveals the joinery and roto hinge placement.

FINAL ASSEMBLY

Begin by gluing up the rabbet joinery in the carcase using hot hide glue. (Whenever a piece has very few parts I use hot hide glue; for more extensive glue-ups, I turn to liquid hide glue for a longer open time.) Then install some bronze ring nails for added strength as well as aesthetic quality.

REINFORCE WITH RING NAILS

After the glue dries, test-fit the drawer. When everything is working as it should, drive some ring nails through the rabbet joints in the

drawer corners. The bronze ring nails add a decorative element to complement the whimsical feel of the multicolored easel surface and the pleasant shape of the walnut shelf. If you use ring nails on your box, make sure you double-check where you're driving them: They're almost impossible to remove.

Along the sides of the carcase, I spaced the nails about 1 in. in from each end and approximately $2\frac{5}{8}$ in. apart. There are 10 per side with 5 down each groove.

1. Cut the two hinge recesses and the groove for the easel legs. 2. An easel shelf gives you a place to rest your sketchbook.

FINISHING TOUCHES

At this point, the pochade box is almost complete, but there are a number of final details you can add that will increase both its utility and its aesthetic appeal.

I attach a leather strap on one end of the box to keep the easel surface in place when transporting it. I screw one end of the leather to the underside of the carcase with a small brass screw and glue an ⅛-in. walnut dowel into a predrilled hole on the top end of the easel surface. I punch a hole in the leather, which wraps around the end of the box to hold everything in place while I'm on the go.

To keep the drawer closed, I install a small ⁵⁄₁₆-in. bullet catch in the bottom of the drawer front. This creates the pressure needed to keep the drawer in place while the box is in motion. Drill a small hole in the underside of one end of the drawer and glue the catch in place.

Furniture tacks make perfect feet for a box this size. Nail four tacks to one side of the box making sure they line up with the carcase top and bottom! You don't want to sink one into

AVAILABLE FROM LEE VALLEY TOOLS AS NOTED

H A R D W A R E

ROTO HINGES ....2 ..... ½ IN. (ITEM #00S01.03)

BULLET CATCH
FOR DRAWER ....1 ..... ⁵⁄₁₆ IN. (ITEM #00G11.50)

BRASS HINGES FOR
SUPPORT ARMS ....2 ..... SMALL

BRONZE RING NAILS ...32....¾ IN. × 14 GAUGE

LEATHER STRAP TO HOLD DRAWER
CLOSED (OPTIONAL) ....1 ..... ⅛ IN. (2 OZ. TO 3 OZ.)
× 1 IN. × 6½ IN.

LEATHER HANDLE
(OPTIONAL) ....1 ..... 9¾ IN. (ITEM # 00S68.01)

the drawer box cavity. On the opposite side of the box I install a leather handle that is held in place with special-purpose brass brackets. They're fastened with four small brass nails.

Between the leather accents and the bronze and brass nails, the pochade box has a flair and style all its own. What's more, it not only keeps my sketching supplies at arm's reach but also inspires me every time I use it. With that, I'm ready to call this project done!

1. Carefully mark the location of the ring nails with an awl and then predrill the holes using a small gimlet. 2. Silicon bronze ring nails will hold this drawer together for years.

A leather strap and a small dowel keep the easel in place while transporting the box.

Install a bullet catch in the drawer front bottom to keep the drawer in place when transporting the box.

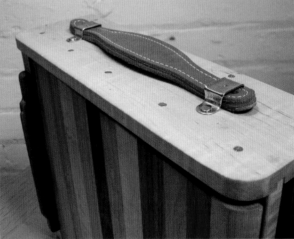

Install a leather handle with brass hardware.

"... my simple message is that if you're going to approach woodworking with sensitivity and maybe refinement, planes are a good way to begin."

—James Krenov

WOOD PLANES

THE RESPONSE you get from a wood plane is altogether different from when you are working with metal handplanes. The tactile feeling absorbed through the sole of a perfectly flattened and polished wooden hand tool you made yourself is a satisfying and liberating experience. Simply put, wood on wood just feels good.

Traditional wood planes are still, after hundreds of years, being manufactured around the world: Old Street Tool, Inc. in the United States, DL Barrett and Sons in Canada, and Philly Planes in the UK are but a few examples. With their detailed mortised throats, this style of plane may seem intimidating for the home woodworker to build. The method I show here is James Krenov's simplified "sandwich" method of wood-plane construction; once you see how straightforward it is, you can adapt it to countless other styles of handplanes, including more traditional forms.

Arguably the most influential figure in modern woodcraft, James Krenov was an author, teacher, cabinetmaker, and champion of the wood planes he used and made

until his passing in 2009. His unique approach and methods of work along with a philosophical view on the craft are still respected, practiced, and taught in woodworking schools around the globe.

The process of making a plane using this method was well documented in Krenov's book *The Fine Art of Cabinetmaking*. Krenov shows the reader the process of making planes using a shop full of power tools, but what about the hand tool–only workshop? Can you build this style handplane without power tools? Without a doubt. Using just a few tools and following a step-by-step process, we'll make high-quality handplanes capable of taking the finest shavings.

RAZEE-STYLE JACK PLANE

A jack plane is one of the most useful tools in the woodshop, capable of taking heavy cuts for dimensioning rough lumber, jointing the edges of stock, and also fine smoothing. If you take care when building the plane and make the sides square to the sole, it can also be used on a shoot-

THE UNPLUGGED WOODSHOP

RAZEE-STYLE
JACK PLANE

SIDE VIEW

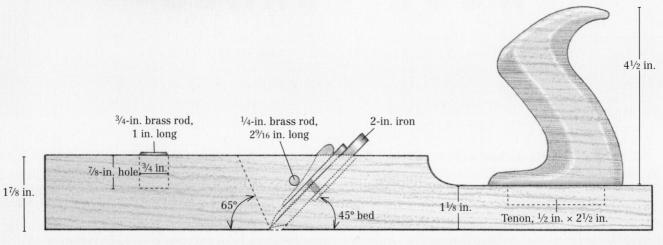

¾-in. brass rod,
1 in. long

¼-in. brass rod,
2⁹⁄₁₆ in. long

2-in. iron

4½ in.

⅞-in. hole   ¾ in.

1⁷⁄₈ in.

65°

45° bed

1⅛ in.

Tenon, ½ in. × 2½ in.

15¾ in.

TOP VIEW

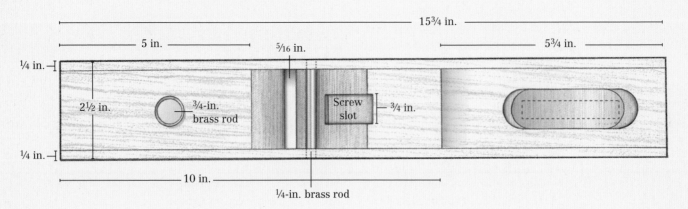

15¾ in.

5 in.

⁵⁄₁₆ in.

5¾ in.

¼ in.

2½ in.   ¾-in.
brass rod

Screw
slot

¾ in.

¼ in.

10 in.

¼-in. brass rod

PLANE BLADES

BLADES FOR the razee jack plane are readily available through mail-order catalogs. Ron Hock in California (www.hocktools.com) started making blades for Krenov's planes in 1981 and is still the leading manufacturer of this style blade and chipbreaker assembly. I wholeheartedly recommend you order a blade from Ron instead of cutting down old stock. The high-carbon tool steel combined with a beautifully mated chipbreaker will lead to positive results and happy shavings.

ing board. A versatile handplane to start with, this jack plane will fill many needs around the woodshop.

The word *razee* or *raze* is said to come from the French word *raser*, meaning "to shave." Throughout history, upper decks on sailing ships were often "razeed," or shaved off, to reduce weight. Similarly, a razee plane is much lighter than a traditional wood plane of equal size due to the removal of the rear section of the plane's body.

PREPARING THE STOCK

You need stable, straight-grained hardwood for any handplane construction, and I decided to go with a piece of the walnut plank I had on hand. If you know ahead of time you're going to build a plane, it's a good idea to let your material sit for a few weeks after you rough-dimension the main pieces. This will allow the wood to acclimatize to your shop.

1. This walnut blank is big enough to make both the jack plane and the smoothing plane. **2.** Crosscut the blank to length and then saw off the two ¼-in. outside cheeks. At this stage, the blank should sit for a few weeks to acclimatize.

If you're using a milder hardwood (one that's less prone to wear resistance) for the plane body, you'll need to laminate a ¼-in. piece of dense hardwood to the sole for added durability. The plane shown here is made from a single block of wood; check the drawing on p. 104 for the correct sizing of the parts.

1. True up the pieces using 220-grit sandpaper on a granite slab. 2. Drill and cut the channel for the cap-screw slot in the blade ramp. 3. Check the fit and make sure the iron lies perfectly flat.

A shopmade miter box will ensure accurate cross-cuts. The two wedges help hold the work.

A SHOPMADE MITER BOX

IF HAND-SAWING isn't your strong point, you can make a simple miter box in just a few minutes that will almost guarantee accurate results. All you need is some 1-in. stock, glue, and a few nails. Carefully lay out the dedicated angles you'll need using the same saw you'll be working with when you saw the blank for the plane. I made this one to accommodate the 45° blade ramp, the 65° front block, and a 50° kerf angle for the high-angle smoother I'll be making next. Throw in a 90° while you're at it for good measure.

MARKING AND SAWING THE BLADE RAMP

Using a shopmade miter box (see the sidebar above), carefully saw the 45° blade ramp and then the 65° front block for the mouth opening (make sure to save the offcut for the wedge!). These pieces should be perfectly square and true. I use some sandpaper on a granite slab to true up any inconsistencies in the blanks (see photo 1 at left) and then finish up with some light cuts with a freshly sharpened low-angle block plane.

Once the blade ramp is true and square, make the channel for the cap-screw slot. Remove the bulk of the material with a bit and refine the cavity with a router plane. Check the fit of the plane iron.

ALIGNING THE PIECES FOR THE CROSS-PIN

The cross-pin and wedge keep the chipbreaker and iron in place while the plane is in use. I made my cross-pin from some ¼-in. brass rod I had in my shop junk drawer; I like the brass rod as it will complement the brass strike button I'll add later on. (You can use wood if you don't have any brass dowel on hand.) The cross-pin should be laid out at 1¼ in. up from the sole and sit about ⅜ in. in front of the chipbreaker (see the drawing on p. 104). Carefully mark the location on the inside of one cheek.

Sandwich the two cheeks together with the outsides facing in and hold them in place with some blue painter's tape while you drill the cross-pin holes (a brad-point bit in a brace makes quick work of this). Fit the brass rod and mark it for length.

ASSEMBLING THE PLANE

With the cross-pin cut and the plane components square and true, go ahead and glue the plane sandwich together. I carefully mark with pencil on the inside of the cheeks where the blade ramp and front block are located. I don't want to get glue inside the throat, although a little squeeze-out isn't a big deal to clean up.

Once the glue is fully cured (about 24 hours if, like me, you're using liquid hide glue), you can remove the clamps and lightly clean up the plane body. I remove the cross-pin and take very light shavings across the body with a jointing plane. Reinstall the cross-pin when complete and fine-tune it (if necessary) for an exact fit.

Now you can make a wedge out of the triangular offcut you saved from sawing the blade ramp earlier . . . you did save it, didn't you? Make the wedge and fine-tune to fit. It should be a good snug fit but not so tight that you have to force it in; light hammer taps should be enough to set it. The front of the wedge is shaped but left rough so it grips a little where it meets the cross-pin. By rough, I mean I leave the scratch marks from my rasp shaping. With the wedge complete, I grab my

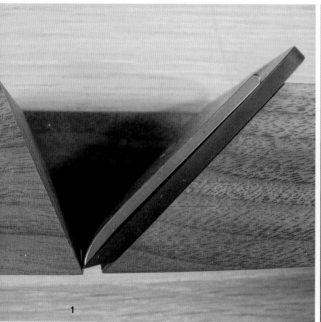

1. Lay out for the cross-pin. 2. Drill the holes in the cheeks, insert the brass rod, and mark it for proper length.

Flatten the sole with a finely tuned jointing plane.

jointing plane and flatten the sole of the plane. If the glue-up went well, this shouldn't be a very long process. A few full shavings and I check the bottom for flat, using a feeler gauge and metal straightedge. Some sandpaper on a flat surface will also help when lapping the sole.

At this point you should have a big, *boring* rectangle of a plane: fully operational but not where I want to leave it. Insert the blade and chipbreaker assembly and test-fit the wedge. Check to make sure the blade is sitting square to the mouth; if any adjustments are needed, now is the time to do so. A fine file is the tool for the job.

RAZEE STYLE

Common complaints I hear about the Krenov-style plane is that it doesn't have a blade adjustment mechanism and there are no "handles" to hold onto. I never had an issue with the lack of mechanical adjustments but can indeed sympathize with those who prefer the feel of a front knob and rear tote.

I use handplanes at every stage of dimensioning lumber so I understand when wood workers say they prefer to have something to hold while flattening large panels or taking heavy cuts when dimensioning rough hardwood. I can get a lot more power behind a plane with a firm grip on a tote and eventually decided to do something about it.

I'm sure if Krenov were here, he'd wrap me across my knuckles with a wooden ruler for this next step. Seriously, you could leave things well enough alone and simply shape the plane to a pleasant profile and get to work. I personally don't like a jack plane without a tote; I use this tool mostly for heavy work and, for me, that means needing something to grip. The razee-style plane, as mentioned in the introduction, is lighter and puts the tote behind the blade, making this a little more comfortable to use (at least in my hands). To begin, I mark off the back portion I wish to remove, and after a few moments with a crosscut saw and a ripsaw, the deed is done. Refine the step-down section with a rasp and file until you're happy with the shape.

MAKING AND INSTALLING THE TOTE

Again, the following steps are highly subjective because everyone has a different preference for the feel of their handplanes. For this one, I decided to go with an open tote, and to begin, I drew the desired shape on a blank of walnut and rough-dimensioned the piece. I resawed the 2-in. stock down to a heavy 1-in. thickness (see photo 1 on p. 110).

A 1-in. auger bit and my favorite brace are the tools of choice for starting the shaping process on the tote. Before I continue shaping the tote, I lay out and saw the tenon in the bottom. This is easier to do now while the piece is still square, and the tenon gives me something to clamp in my vise while I'm shaping the piece. Fine-tune the tenon and then get back to

1. To create a razee-style plane, begin by removing the back section. 2. Refine the curve with a half-round rasp.

1. Resaw the blank stock for the rear tote. The second line underneath the tote marks the tenon that will be mortised into the rear of the plane body. 2. Use an auger bit to establish the round areas of the tote. 3. Cut the tenon while the piece is still square. 4. The tenon provides a grip for the vise while shaping the tote. 5. Finish up with some light sanding.

shaping the tote. After a series of sawcuts it's on to the rasp and file work to refine the shape. Finish up with some light sanding.

Now you're ready to lay out a mortise in the center back section of the body. I removed the bulk of the material with a brace and bit and squared off the mortise with some chisel work. After any necessary fine-tuning, glue the tote into the mortise. Let the glue set and, once dry, apply a good coat of boiled linseed oil to the entire plane. Then it's over to the sharpening bench to sharpen and polish the iron before making the first few passes.

FINISHING TOUCHES

On my initial test-drive, the plane swept cleanly across a piece of cherrywood taking a substantial shaving. There was no chatter or tearing, but only that sweet, high-pitched whistle you get from a freshly sharpened iron set in a finely tuned handplane. I reset the blade to try a finer cut. Again, that beautiful sound and a fine curl of cherry lifted from the mouth. I really like the feel of this plane. It is lightweight, well balanced, and easy to use.

ETCH WITH GARLIC

TIP

Here's a little trick for anytime you're gluing metal components with hot hide glue. Take a fresh clove of garlic, cut it open, and rub the clove on the metal parts before you glue them in place. The oil from the freshly cut garlic will lightly etch the brass and help the glue bond better. It really works!

Lay out the mortise on the back of the plane, remove the bulk of the material with an auger bit, and then use chisels to bring the mortise square.

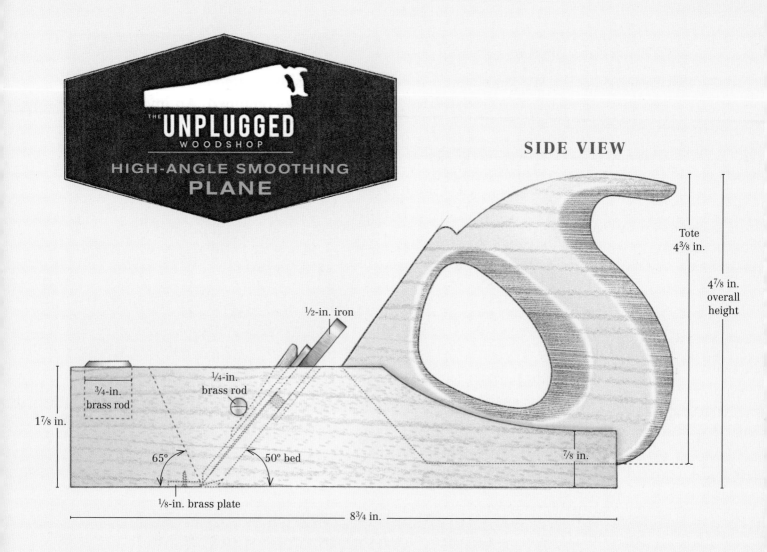

SIDE VIEW

Tote
4³⁄₈ in.

4⁷⁄₈ in.
overall
height

¹⁄₂-in. iron

¹⁄₄-in.
brass rod

³⁄₄-in.
brass rod

1⁷⁄₈ in.

65°

50° bed

7⁄₈ in.

¹⁄₈-in. brass plate

8³⁄₄ in.

TOP VIEW

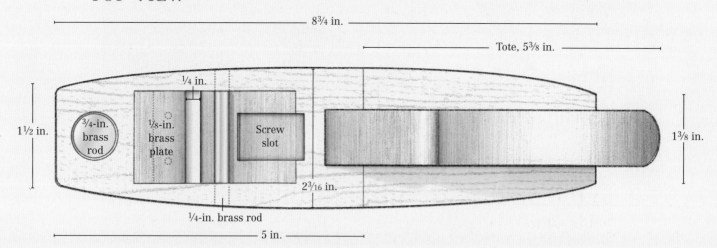

8³⁄₄ in.

Tote, 5³⁄₈ in.

¹⁄₄ in.

1¹⁄₂ in.

³⁄₄-in.
brass
rod

¹⁄₈-in.
brass
plate

Screw
slot

1³⁄₈ in.

2³⁄₁₆ in.

¹⁄₄-in. brass rod

5 in.

The finished jack plane, with front strike button installed.

All planes made in this style are adjusted with light hammer taps. In use, you may find the wood will get dents and bruises over time, so I install a front strike button in the front. This is simply a ¾-in. piece of brass dowel crosscut to 1 in. and glued in a hole drilled in the center of the plane about a 1½ in. forward of the throat opening.

Hit the strike button when you want to retract the iron and/or remove the wedge and iron assembly. To advance the iron, lightly tap the end with a small hammer until the desired projection is achieved. You may find this process a little alien at first, but after a bit of practice, it will become second nature.

Give the plane another light coat of oil, finish with some wax, and you're ready to go to work.

HIGH-ANGLE SMOOTHING PLANE

Most handplanes come with a blade bedded at 45°. This standard, or *common*, angle is suitable for many applications, but a high-angle plane will tame the most difficult wood grain and is a great addition to your kit. With the razee-style jack and this high-angle smoother, you'll be able to tackle most of your woodshop planing needs. The process of making this or any other Krenov-style handplane is the same as described in the previous section. I added a few details to this smoother and will highlight them as we go.

BEGIN WITH THE BLANK

My method for sawing the block, once it's flat and square, is to begin by marking and sawing off one cheek at a thickness of about ⁵⁄₁₆ in. Plane both of the sawn surfaces to remove any sawmarks and then mark the middle block using the blade/chipbreaker assembly as reference for your marking gauge (see the top photo on p. 114). Make the middle section about ⅛ in. wider than the overall width of the blade so you'll be able to adjust it laterally while in use. Saw the middle section and again remove the sawmarks before continuing. Mark the second cheek using the width of the first as reference and saw it out.

The razee plane (background) is ideal for flattening the parts of the high-angle smoother (foreground).

SAWING THE BLADE RAMP AND FRONT BLOCK

After sawing the blank for the plane body, saw the blade ramp at an angle of 50°; this angle was popular in early English infill planes like the much sought after Norris planes and is often referred to as a *York pitch*. The front ramp

Saw the blade ramp to 50°.

angle is kept the same as the jack plane and is cut at 65°. Use the shopmade miter box for accuracy in the crosscuts (see p. 106).

INSTALLING THE THROAT PLATE

One of the few differences between this plane and the jack, other than the overall size and shape, is an added brass insert in the throat. The throat insert helps the plane wear better and is installed in the front middle block before the plane pieces are glued up.

Set your marking gauge using the brass throat insert and scribe the width and depth of the brass stock on the bottom of the front block. Define the area with a crosscut saw and use a router plane to remove the material. Next drill some screw holes in both the brass insert and the plane body. Glue and screw the plate in place, with the screw heads left proud of the plane bottom. These will get filed off after the glue is set and the block is flattened and carefully filed so the brass insert is absolutely flush with the sides and front of the block.

1. Crosscut the front block to establish a ⅛-in. recess for the brass plate. 2. Use a router plane to remove the waste to an accurate depth. 3. Predrill the brass plate and the front block. 4. Glued and screwed . . . the screws will be filed flush with the plane bottom. 5. True the blank on sticky-backed sandpaper applied to granite slab. 6. Check the fit.

1. Cut the rear slope. 2. Establish the handle profile using paper patterns. 3. Glue the pattern directly to the walnut blank and establish the round sections of the tote with an auger bit. 4. Refine the shape with a bowsaw. 5. Remove the waste in the rear mortise.

BLADE RAMP DETAILS AND GLUE-UP

Once the brass insert is complete and you've done a dry-fit, continue along with the same basic steps I covered for making the jack plane: flattening the blade ramp, cutting out the cap-screw slot, marking and drilling the cross-pin, and then gluing the plane.

FINE-TUNING THE MOUTH

Once the glue-up is complete, remove the clamps and flatten the sole of the plane using sandpaper on a granite slab. Then true the mouth of the plane, giving careful attention to the opening. I keep the mouth much tighter on this high-angle smoother for the lightest shavings to pass through.

SHAPING THE PLANE AND INSTALLING THE TOTE

At this stage again, the plane is ready to work, but I decided to carry on and shape the body, making a closed tote for the back and rounding the sides of the plane to give it a coffin shape. You can shape the plane to whatever suits your style; there is no right or wrong here. This

Fine-tuned and ready for shaping.

plane was inspired by the infill planes of old with their high-angle York pitch, so I chose to shape this one to reflect that same tradition of English-style plane making, as shown in the photos on the facing page.

I do a bit more rounding on the front and install a brass strike button centered in the front top, using the same drill and glue method described on p. 113. Give the plane body a final rub with some 220-grit sandpaper and then apply a few coats of oil and finally some wax. Before use, lap the sole using sandpaper on a granite block until it's dead flat. Install a freshly sharpened iron and you're done.

Test-driving the new smoother on some difficult-grain mahogany.

"As long as there are men who have not forgotten
how to work with their hands,
there will remain for the heritage of the craftsman
a bright light of hope
that began at the dawn of civilization."

—Sam Maloof

KERFING PLANE

NECESSITY WAS truly the mother of invention for this invaluable tool. The first project I built for this book was the gentleman's valet (see p. 166). As you'll see when you get to that chapter, I used a piece of holly to make the drawer pull. This was the first time I had used holly in an application that did not involve stringing or banding.

I was really excited about how the holly worked and finished and thought it would be nice to make an entire cabinet out of it. I had only the one plank of holly, so I'd either be building a very small box, or I could resaw it into ⅛-in.-thick sheets of veneer and make a slightly larger piece. Choosing the veneer option, I needed to figure out the best way to resaw the holly using only hand tools.

With help from Mark Harrell, the man behind Bad Axe Tool Works™ (www.badaxetoolworks. com), I started trying a few different configurations of custom sawblades for the frame-saw design I had been developing (see p. 134). But even with a frame saw, handsawing accurate ⅛-in. veneer is still a challenge. I needed something that would make this system a little more foolproof.

A handsaw will always follow the path of least resistance, so I thought if I could somehow establish this path, I wouldn't have any problems with saw drift. My first instinct was to use a plow plane. If I could plow a thin groove around the edge of a plank before resawing, then perhaps the sawblade would follow it. I grabbed my small Veritas® plow plane and fitted it with its narrowest ⅛-in. cutter. Too wide. I thought about grinding the plow-plane iron down until it was just slightly wider than the thickness of the sawblade. Too fragile and hard to resharpen.

Then the light bulb went on, and I realized that the answer was to install a sawblade instead of the plane iron. The first few prototypes (there are eight of them so far) had fixed fences and were rectangular in shape, much like a traditional wooden molding plane. They worked for sawing a kerf but weren't all that comfortable for sawing long board edges. So I shaped the body with a more comfortable grip and came up with a few new profiles, which eventually became a marriage between a handsaw and a handplane tote.

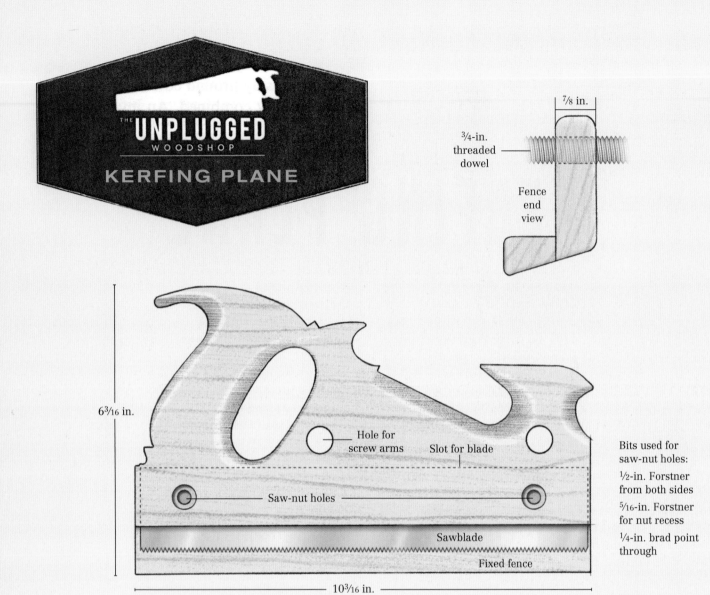

THE **UNPLUGGED** WOODSHOP

KERFING PLANE

7/8 in.

3/4-in. threaded dowel

Fence end view

6³/₁₆ in.

Hole for screw arms

Slot for blade

Saw-nut holes

Sawblade

Fixed fence

Bits used for saw-nut holes:

1/2-in. Forstner from both sides

5/16-in. Forstner for nut recess

1/4-in. brad point through

10³/₁₆ in.

ADJUSTABLE FENCE

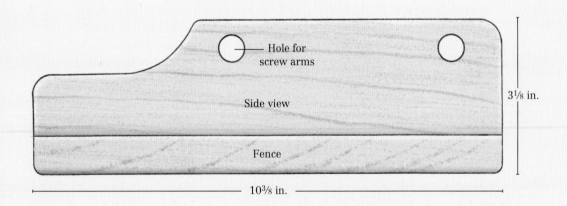

Hole for screw arms

Side view

Fence

3¹/₈ in.

10³/₈ in.

In use, the fixed fence kerfing plane works and feels a little bit like a molding plane.

And so the kerfing plane was born. This new tool is basically a wooden plane and a ripsaw combined. It allows you to easily and effortlessly saw a kerf at ⅛ in. off the face of a board; once the kerf is established, you drop the blade of a frame saw down into it. Once you start sawing, you'll quickly find that the pre-established kerfs down the edges of a board will guide the frame-saw blade, resulting in more accurate sawcuts without ever having to worry about saw drift or sawing off a line. If you use a well-made sawblade, for both the kerfing plane and the frame saw, resawing in a hand tool–only workshop just got a whole lot easier!

THE FIXED-FENCE MODEL

The first kerfing plane model I'll demonstrate making has a fixed fence set at ⅛ in. It's the tool to use if you want a dedicated plane for one specific job. The second version has an adjustable fence much like a traditional wooden plow plane. It's a wonderful multipurpose tool, but

some people don't like having to adjust a fence. You need to set it before a cut and make sure it doesn't move while in use. With a fixed-fence version, there is never a doubt of the fence moving: It's reliable and accurate, but it can do only one job.

PREPARING THE STOCK

There is very little material invested in a fixed-fence kerfing plane. You'll need a 1-in.-thick piece of stable stock, 10³⁄₁₆ in. long and 6³⁄₁₆ in.

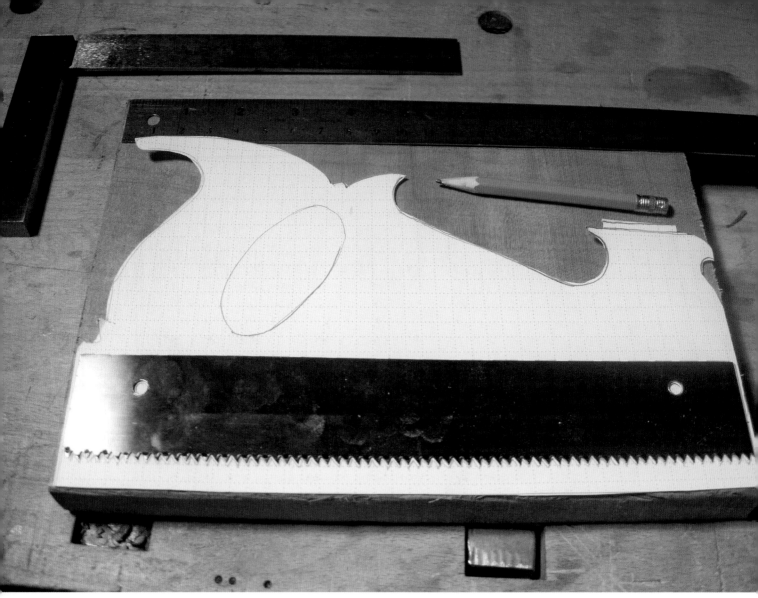

Make an accurate template indicating the key locations: the rabbet, saw slot, and saw-nut locations. The final shape can be whatever you like.

wide. Quartersawn hardwood is the only material I would suggest using on this tool for reasons of stability and longevity.

The first step is to create a full-size, paper template, which is critical for accurate layout. Be sure to mark the key locations of the template, including the rabbet, the saw slot, and the saw-nut locations.

CUTTING THE RABBET

Dimension the stock to size (I used quarter-sawn cherry for the plane body), check it for square, and then lay out the rabbet on the plane sole. Use a moving fillister or side rabbet plane to remove the bulk of the waste in the rabbet. I tend to switch from a side rabbet to a

Scribe a line for the rabbet as deep as the marking gauge allows, establishing a crisp edge where the material needs to be removed. The rabbet measures $3/8$ in. wide by $15/16$ in. deep.

1. A shoulder plane is great for creeping up to the scribe lines of the rabbet. 2. Check for square as you work.

I used a large ripsaw for cutting the slot. You can see the blue painter's tape holding the ⅛-in. shim in place as I saw.

large shoulder plane for more control as I creep up on the scribe lines.

The shoulder plane seems to have better sight lines, making it easier to keep scribe lines in tact right up until that final one thousandth of an inch pass. It can also make precision cuts

right into the corner. A large backsaw may also work for cutting the rabbet, again, followed by some light handplane work to finish. Like most things in woodworking, there's always more than one option. Bottom line, cut the rabbet and make it square!

SAWING THE BLADE SLOT

For the next step, you'll need a reliable back-saw with a rip tooth. Mark the depth of the cut and the distance from the inside of the fence. This kerfing plane will have a set width for a cut that's ⅛ in. off the fence, which is a good general thickness for bent lamination work, shopmade veneer, and stringing. Use a wide chisel to cut a shallow shoulder that defines the scribe line while sawing the plate slot. This V-groove will help the sawteeth bite in exactly where you want them to.

The sawcut is critical and should be absolutely square to the fence. It will determine the location of the blade and, in turn, the thickness of the cuts you'll be able to make, so make sure it goes exactly where you want it. To make the sawcut a little easier, temporarily attach an ⅛-in.-thick shim to the fence as a saw guide. Saw the kerf into the plane bottom with your saw pressed up against the shim and eye the depth as you go.

Carefully saw down to, but not over, the depth line and test-fit the blade in the slot. The last few saw strokes should be executed in a way so that the teeth are no longer cutting but you're only clearing away the waste for the saw plate to have an easier entrance. With the saw-plate slot complete, you're ready to drill the saw-nut holes.

INSTALLING THE BLADE

Double-check that the saw-nut locations are properly marked on both sides of the plane body (you'll be drilling in from both sides). Using two Forstner bits and a brad-point bit, drill the required holes for the saw nuts, as shown in the photos on p. 124.

For the saw plate (blade), you can salvage an old panel saw or shape a shiny piece of new steel. If your saw-making skills are up to it, then look at the specs and grab a couple of saw

1. Drill a hole using a ½-in. Forstner bit on both sides of the plane body; the holes are made to the exact depth of the saw-nut heads. 2. Check the depth as you go. The first step on the head of the saw nut should sit flush on both sides of the plane body. 3. For the second step of the saw nut, use a ⁵⁄₁₆-in. Forstner bit to drill a hole on one side only: the outside of the plane body. 4. From the *business*, or blade, side of the plane, use a ¼-in. brad-point bit to complete the hole. Test-fit the nuts and fine-tune if necessary.

nuts while you're at it. My saw-making skills still have a ways to go, so I asked Mark Harrell at Bad Axe Tool Works to make some saw plates for me. I recommend you do the same (see Resources on p. 230). Mark has made a few different saw plates for me, with different plate thicknesses, tooth counts, and configurations. I think he nailed it on this one for both speed and function: It is a hybrid tooth filed at 5 ppi (points per inch).

SHAPING THE BODY

With the blade installed, the plane is ready to function. You could chamfer the edges of the body and test-drive the tool, but I opted to refine the profile on the one shown here. Before you begin the shaping, remove the blade and transfer the template onto the stock.

Remove the larger curved areas first using a ¾-in. and 1-in. bit. I use my brace and bit and drill in from both sides of the body, meeting in the middle and reducing the chance of blowout (see the photos on p. 126). From here, move onto the rasps, files, scrapers, and finally sandpaper, until you're satisfied with the shape. Check often to feel the tote in hand as you work, and allow the plane body to form to the shape of your hands.

FINISHING UP

Once the shaping is complete, finish as you see fit. I used a few coats of oil finish; you might want to apply some wax after a bit of use. Reinstall the blade and take some test cuts. Take note of the movement and check to see that the blade is running parallel to the fence. If it isn't, you'll notice right away that the kerf is wider than it should be. If that's the case, make another test cut to confirm that you weren't holding the tool away from the work. If it happens on the second try, then you'll have to adjust the fence. You can't change the plate slot location, but you can take a micro shav-

Install the blade in the slot and line up the holes using an awl to help position the saw-nut locations. Insert the nuts to lock the blade in place.

ing or two off the fence to square things up. If it's off the other way, you may have to glue on a shim and reshape the rabbet square to the plate slot. Or this may be a good time to plane off the existing fence and make yourself a kerfing plane with an adjustable fence!

The saw plate and fence need to be as close to parallel as possible. Check that the depth of the blade protrudes consistently from the plane sole.

1. To reduce the risk of blowout when shaping the body, stop about halfway through and finish drilling the holes from the opposite side.
2. Make straight sawcuts to rough out the shape. 3. Finish the inside curves with a bowsaw. 4. Pencil in details as you work your way down to the desired shape. A few sawcuts help define the shape at this transition. 5. Use small files between the "nostrils"; the manufactured width dictates this part of the design. 6. Take the ornamentation as far as you'd like or leave it unrefined and utilitarian. Whatever feels best in your hand when you pick it up to work—that above all else, should dictate the final shape.

USING THE KERFING PLANE

WHEN USING THE kerfing plane, begin by taking a light pass along the edge of the work. This is to set up both your brain and your arms and to give you a quick look at the placement of the kerf. Make sure those three things are all good and, beginning at the end of the workpiece, start sawing in the kerf. I tend to rest my thumb in the low part of the toe and my fingers at the bottom of the fence when getting started.

Use your forward hand to keep the fence square and held tight to the workpiece, while you place your other hand on the rear tote and use it to push the plane forward. Work your way toward the back of the piece. When the plane bottoms out you're done! If you're using wet wood, stop and clear the sawdust off the teeth every few passes.

The plane is comfortable in use and saws quickly and accurately to depth.

THE ADJUSTABLE-FENCE MODEL

Adding an adjustable fence will enable one plane body to cut any set width of material thickness to the given depth of the saw plate. The one shown here will saw kerfs up to an offset of $2\frac{3}{8}$ in., but you could add longer arms for a wider offset, which might be particularly useful for dado work inside cabinets. The entire conversion took me the morning.

Begin by carefully laying out the screw holes in the plane body (see "Kerfing Plane" on p. 120). Bore and tap the holes using a $\frac{3}{4}$-in. wood-threading tool (see p. 79). The $\frac{3}{4}$-in. tap requires a $\frac{5}{8}$-in. hole. Next thread the screw arms, which are made from 6-in.-long, $\frac{3}{4}$-in. dowel. I allow the cherry dowel to soak overnight in some boiled linseed oil before cutting the threads with a dedicated thread-cutting tool. Check the fit and clean up the ends of the screws.

Now make the four wooden bolts. I used some 5/4 flat-sawn cherry that I had on hand in my country shop but will make four more from some quartersawn stock I have back in the city shop. The bolts don't have to be perfect circles! It's the inside that matters. After the bolts are drilled and shaped, tap the holes and test them on the threaded arms.

MAKING THE FENCE

If you're converting the standard kerfing plane we just built over to a kerfing plane with adjustable fence, you first need to remove the existing fixed fence (take a deep breath!). I used a ripsaw to remove the fence and squared up the plane bottom with a jack plane. If you're making the adjustable fence model from scratch, saw the saw slot into the plane bottom (see photo 3 below). You could size a block of wood to serve as a fence when you saw.

Make the fence in two parts using a stable hardwood (I had an offcut of mahogany that I used for this one). The larger piece for the fence body is dimensioned to $10\frac{3}{8}$ in. long by $3\frac{1}{8}$ in. wide by $\frac{7}{8}$ in. thick. The second, smaller part forms the lower block on the fence and is dimensioned to $10\frac{3}{8}$-in. long by $\frac{7}{8}$ in. wide by $\frac{3}{4}$ in. thick.

1. Two wooden screws are threaded into holes drilled and tapped into the side of the kerfing plane. The adjustable fence will slide in and out on these. 2. Make the four wooden bolts that thread onto the screw arm. Flatten the sides on a piece of sandpaper. 3. If necessary, remove the fixed fence from the kerfing plane and plane the bottom square to the side.

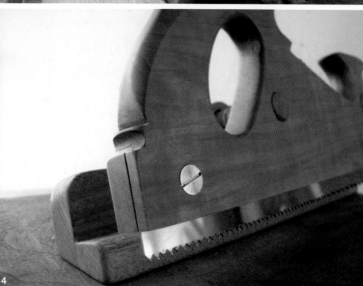

1. Crosscuts make removing the waste area of the fence easier. 2. After the fence is complete, reinstall the saw plate and install the new fence. 3. I use a small wood and brass hammer to tap the fence into position—similar to adjusting a wooden plane iron with a wedge. Set the bolts close and gently tap the fence to the final width of cut desired. 4. Ready for the first test-drive. The bottom bevel on the new fence makes for a perfect stand!

The two fence parts are dimensioned, jointed, and glued together to create the lower part of the fence. The dimensions aren't critical. The fence could be made slightly shorter or longer, depending on what feels good in your hand. A longer fence will give you more surface to register along the workpiece, which may be beneficial. The lower outside edge of the fence is beveled, and the side of the fence is shaped to match the rear tote on the plane body, which gives more room for your fingers. Many traditional wooden plow planes have wide, decorative moldings for these fence parts. This may be an option for you and would certainly elevate the aesthetic of the design.

Now about that frame saw . . .

With the fence set at $\frac{1}{8}$ in. from the saw plate, I'm processing the plank of holly used in the medicine chest project (see p. 140).

"The details are not the details,
they make the design."

—Charles Eames

FRAME SAW

A FRAME SAW is a wonderful addition to the hand tool–only woodshop. When used in combination with a kerfing plane (see p. 118), you can resaw stock down to $\frac{1}{8}$ in. in thickness. Wider cuts, in stock up to the inside width of the saw frame, are also possible and, in some situations, easier than when using a traditional handsaw (ripping thick timber comes to mind). The thin sawblade, in this case $2\frac{1}{16}$ in. wide, is captured under tension in a balanced, hardwood frame. This narrow plate makes it easy to move the saw through the most difficult material, offering much less resistance than a traditional handsaw.

The saw frame I've designed is a modern version of the traditional saw design with the biggest difference being size; the second being a handlebar-style grip.

Let's get started.

PREPARING THE HARDWARE

Begin this project by selecting the hardware. If you know a local blacksmith in your community, this hardware could be as elaborate as you'd like. For this example, I'm using off-the-shelf supplies.

I purchased a short length of 2-in. by 4-in. rectangular tubing from a local metal supplier and had them crosscut two pieces at $1\frac{1}{8}$ in. in width. (That part of the job cost about the price of a cup of coffee.) Clean away any sharp burrs along the edges and scratch a center line at one end of each piece that will give you a cut depth of about $1\frac{5}{8}$ in. Refer to the drawing for details.

Slow, steady strokes are essential when you begin to saw the plate slot. A sharp hacksaw will cut through the $\frac{1}{8}$-in. steel tubing without any trouble. Saw as straight as you can down the scribe lines. (You could also ask the metal supplier to cut the slots for you.) Use a metal file and clear away any burrs left behind from the hacksaw cut.

Check again to see if the kerf is as straight as you could make it. If the plate slot isn't perfectly straight, you may see small deflections in the blade once the saw is finished and under working tension. It's not the end of the world. If, however, the kerf is really out of square and you

FRONT BRACKET

(FRONT VIEW) (SIDE VIEW)

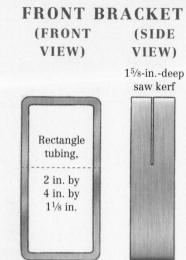

1⅝-in.-deep saw kerf

Rectangle tubing, 2 in. by 4 in. by 1⅛ in.

FRONT FRAME ARM (TOP VIEW)

¾ in.

The corner holes are drilled with a #13 by 13⁄16-in. bit.

Retaining pins, 3⁄16-in. rod

FRONT FRAME ARM (FRONT VIEW)

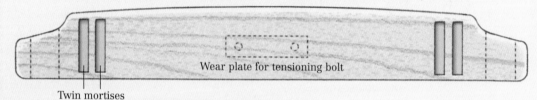

Twin mortises

Wear plate for tensioning bolt

BACK HANDLEBAR (TOP VIEW)

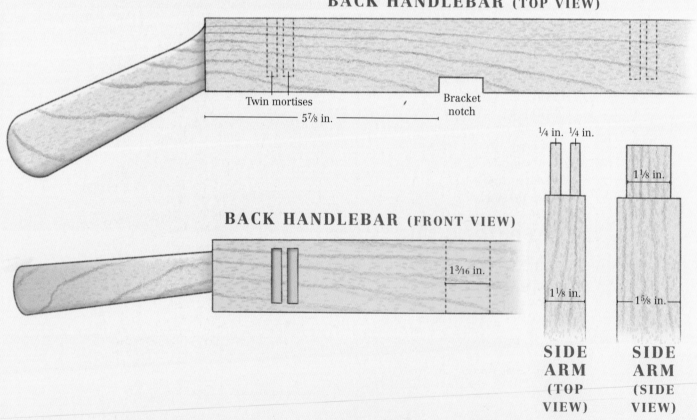

Twin mortises

Bracket notch

5⅞ in.

BACK HANDLEBAR (FRONT VIEW)

1³⁄16 in.

¼ in. ¼ in.

1⅛ in.

1⅛ in.

1⅝ in.

SIDE ARM (TOP VIEW)

SIDE ARM (SIDE VIEW)

1. Establish a square kerf across the end of the rectangular tubing. 2. Stop when you reach the desired 1⅝ in. depth.

notice it is affecting the cut, get a new piece of tubing and start over.

I bought the ³⁄₁₆-in. steel rod for the retaining pins from the local hardware store for a few dollars. You can leave it long for now because the extra length will make it easier to bend. Bend the rod and test-fit that both ends will fit through the holes in the saw plate. With a little trial and error, you should be able to bend a couple of snug-fitting retaining pins (see photo 1 on p. 134).

I used an off-the-shelf, ⅜-in. eye bolt and nut for the tensioning bolt. Drill a hole centered on the end of one of the brackets for the bolt; the nut is threaded on the inside of the bracket until there's about ¾ in. showing. When the

Test-fit the saw plate in the bracket.

frame is assembled and the saw plate starts to tighten, the nut will push on the bracket and tighten up the saw plate. File the rectangular tubing and sand away any sharp edges. After a quick coat with some metal spray paint, you're good to go.

You'll also need a small metal wear plate that the tensioning screw will press into while in use. The one I used is $3/16$ in. thick, $1/2$ in. wide, and 2 in. long; it came already countersunk.

1. Bend the steel rod for the retaining pins using a metal bending jig. (This one is available from Lee Valley Tools.) 2. The frame saw hardware ready for the frame.

Working from the cut list and drawing, dimension the frame parts.

FRAME-SAW BLADE

THERE'S ALWAYS some give and take when it comes to the hand tools we make in our home shops. Through the years, I've tried using everything for frame-saw blades from mutilated panel saw plates I had cut down into thin strips to old bandsaw blades stretched between a basic wooden frame. Technically, they all worked and will rip up wood in a hurry; but they offer poor control, with very little feedback.

The saw plate I used for this frame saw is one Mark Harrell of Bad Axe Tool Works (www.badaxetoolworks.com) made for me. It's 0.025-gauge steel and is filed at 6 ppi (points per inch) making it easy to move and control. Using a custom-shaped frame saw, with handles carefully shaped to your own hands, plus a professionally manufactured sawblade, will elevate your resawing experience and inspire you to undertake woodworking techniques you never thought possible in a hand tool-only woodshop.

BUILDING THE WOODEN FRAME

Turning to the frame itself, work from the cut list and drawing to dimension the four wooden parts. Once the stock is prepared, cut the double tenons and mortises as shown in the photos on the facing page.

With the frame dry-fit, measure and mark where the brackets go. The front and rear frame parts will be shaped, but the area under the brackets should be left rectangular in shape.

Next lay out the handle grips. Note that the grips splay out on both the horizontal and

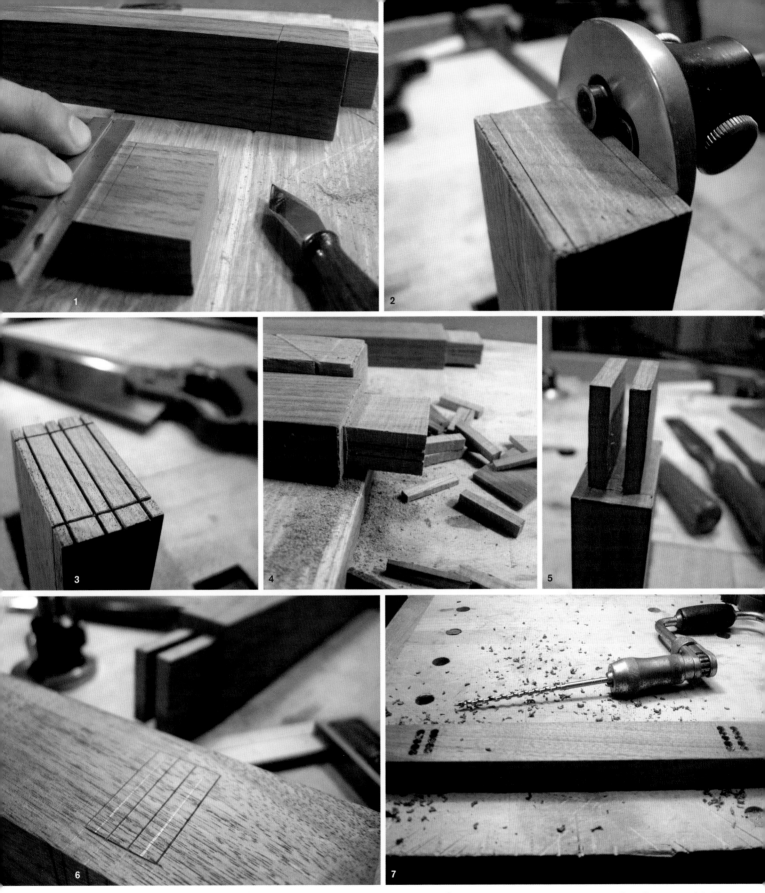

1. Scribe the depth of the shoulders for the double tenons on the ends of the arms. 2. Mark the widths and cheeks on the tenons. 3. Saw the tenons. A half dozen rip cuts later, it's over to the bench hook for crosscutting the shoulders. 4. Crosscut your way around the shoulders. I tend to leave a little fat and prefer to chisel away those final few shavings. 5. Saw away the waste between the tenons with a fretsaw and then clean the shoulders down to the scribe lines with a chisel. Finish off the arms and move onto the mortises. 6. Pencil in the joinery on the front frame and handlebar and define the lines with a crisp scribe line. Some prefer to scribe the entire mortise, others only one side, whatever method you choose is fine. 7. Bore away the waste with a ¼-in. bit and clean up with a chisel. Fine-tune the mortises and test-fit the frame.

vertical axis. When you're holding them in a day or two from now, resawing some lumber, you'll appreciate the shaping you did; if there's an area you're going to spend an extra hour on, it should be here. Working between the bench hook and bench vise, saw away the waste to reveal the handlebar grips.

The back handlebar frame should be notched for the rear plate bracket to keep the bracket centered in use. Refer to "Frame Saw" on p. 132 for the location of the notch. Make a few crosscuts and then remove the waste with a large chisel. Clean up the area with some final paring cuts and test-fit the bracket.

INSTALLING THE WEAR PLATE

The front wear plate mortise should be cut before you begin any shaping. Scribe the plate location on the front center of the frame and begin removing the waste with a series of shallow chisel blows. The final depth can be refined with a router plane, working in from both ends.

TIP

Make sure to shape the grips to fit your own hands! The specs given here fit mine. For that matter, make a template of the handlebar grip and adjust it so it's the same width as your shoulders if it feels better. This one suits my "frame" just fine.

Use a center punch and countersink before fastening the wear plate.

CURVING THE FRAME ENDS

I put comfortable handle grips pretty high up on my design detail list. Also a "round" or curved detail at the front was important to me. Feel free to use any carved embellishment you want here. Eager to get back to work, I added a quick corner detail inspired by the curved sweep on traditional frame saws, drilling a $^{13}/_{16}$-in.-dia. hole through the corner and scal-

Lay out the handle grips.

1. Small bites and light taps are all that's needed for the shallow mortise for the wear plate. 2. Checking the fit. My mortise is a hair wide but that's only cosmetics. 3. I used a French curve to design a basic corner shape for the front arm. Make a full-size paper template and transfer the round corner shapes onto the frame. 4. Bore the holes with a brace and bit and then rough out the shape with a series of sawcuts. Use rasps and files, scrapers and sandpaper to refine the desired shape.

loping the top. It adds a visual detail to finish off the front of the frame, but more important, it reduces the weight of the saw a little. If you think you'll be using the saw with a partner, then make two handlebar ends instead. Same joinery, just different profiles.

SHAPING THE HANDLES

Mark the handle grips with dividers and file away the corners. Much like shaping the kerfing plane (see p. 124), stop every few minutes and hold the tool in your hands. Close your eyes. You'll know when the shaping is done.

File away the corners of the handlebar grips and refine to the desired shape.

Make the grips as comfortable as possible and you'll get many hours of use out of this fine hand tool.

After shaping and sanding, apply a generous coat of oil/varnish. Allow the finish to rest for an hour and then wipe away the excess. Apply as many coats as you like and finish with a final wipe of steel wool and citrus wax for that smooth and silky feeling.

ASSEMBLING THE SAW

Slide the brackets onto each end of the frame, making sure that the bracket with the ³⁄₈-in. hole is toward the front and centered on the wear plate. Insert the eyebolt through the hole and thread the nut onto the end. Connect the frame arms and squeeze the joinery together (and rejoice that there's no glue required!). Press the saw plate into the plate slots on the brackets and install the ³⁄₁₆-in. U-shaped retaining pins through the holes in each end of the saw plate.

BRACE AND BIT CAN'T BE BEAT

OLD BRACES AND BITS are extremely efficient tools for drilling holes or boring away waste for joinery. I see them all the time at antiques dealers and at hand-tool trade shows. If you haven't done so already, pick some up for yourself. I can't fathom why the current hand tool manufacturers aren't offering any modern interpretations of the brace and bit. Hint, hint . . . Oh yes, the cordless drill. Right.

1. Properly seated, the ³⁄₁₆-in. retaining pins hold the saw plate tight against the bracket end wall. 2. The front tensioning bolt is all lined up with wear plate. I left the bolt long for now, but if you like you can trim it down to about 1½ in. of threads in length. The longer bolt just makes it a little easier to grip while tightening. 3. The side arms are rounded and shaped so the union between the two parts is protected but softened.

All ready to resaw. Are you?

TENSIONING THE BLADE

Lay the saw safely on a flat surface with the teeth facing down (for safety). You'll need to shim the frame up a little so the blade can hang down below the frame bottom by ½ in. or so.

Extend the end of the eyebolt over the edge of the work surface and begin turning it until the blade feels taught in hand with a spring-back of no more than ⅛ in. at most. If you feel or see any movement in the frame, stop. If you're joinery isn't accurate, you'll notice it now. Make any adjustments and tighten the saw plate to working tension. As you tighten the saw frame, check that the corners of the frame remain flat on your benchtop. Note if there's any twist or wind and try to determine the misfit corner where the joinery may need some more refining.

The kerfing plane and frame saw are a great duo worth spending the time to make. These tools will open an entirely new world of possibilities in the hand-tool woodshop. Explore their potential and, more important, have some fun with them!

⇥ FOR YOUR SAFETY ⇤

I plan on making a few different frames with varying sizes, saw plates, and grip variations. Hand tools are constantly being reinvented and evolve to suit both the user and the application. Before altering any existing designs make sure to test the frame strength and the saw plates you use. A saw plate tensioned between a wooden frame has the potential to be an accident waiting to happen. Work safely.

TIP

THE
GOOD DOCTOR'S
MEDICINE
CHEST

"Forgive me, but I'm forced to take unusual precautions."

—Dr. Henry Frankenstein

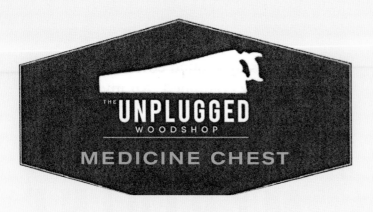

MEDICINE CHEST

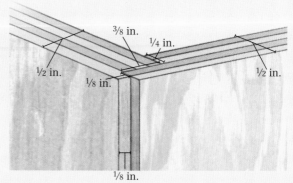

³⁄₈ in.

¹⁄₄ in.

¹⁄₂ in.

¹⁄₈ in.

¹⁄₂ in.

¹⁄₈ in.

WINDOW PATTERN

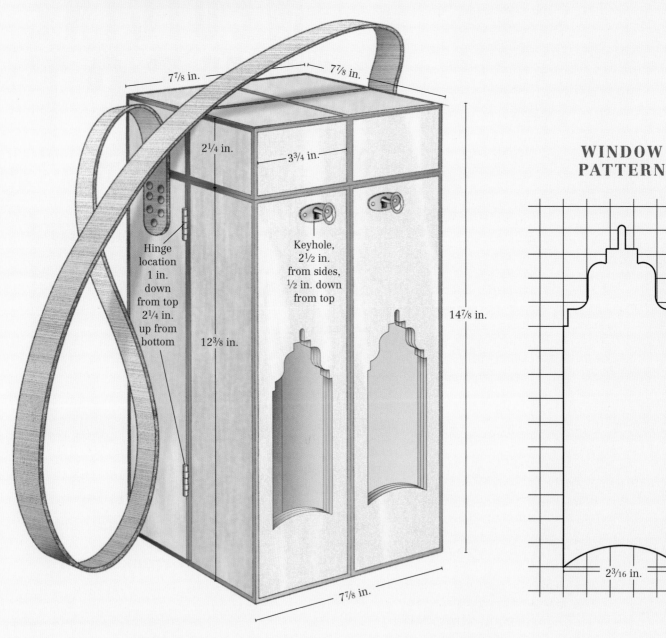

7⁷⁄₈ in.

7⁷⁄₈ in.

2¹⁄₄ in.

3³⁄₄ in.

Hinge location 1 in. down from top 2¹⁄₄ in. up from bottom

Keyhole, 2¹⁄₂ in. from sides, ¹⁄₂ in. down from top

14⁷⁄₈ in.

12³⁄₈ in.

7⁷⁄₈ in.

6¹⁄₈ in.

2³⁄₁₆ in.

Finished back view of chest.

IN THE DAYS BEFORE corner drugstores and today's big-box pharmaceutical emporiums, the medicine chest was the way medical practitioners would transport their goods. From weird and wonderful to eccentric and essential, the contents of the medicine chest included potions, ointments, and no doubt a good dose of snake oil too. With examples dating from the 1500s all the way up through the 1800s, we can find many amazing versions of these fine little boxes.

We don't see medicine chests per se in use anymore, but these intricate boxes make for enjoyable projects that can be adapted for a variety of modern-day uses. A very good friend of mine is a self-proclaimed oenophile, and my version of this case will be a perfect tote for him to transport a few bottles of his finest stock.

Resawn holly will be put to good use here, while the leather interior with walnut accents and quality brass hardware mixes media to create a unique style. Filled with spirits, wines, vinegars, or olive oil, the good doctor's medicine chest will open the door to your imagination.

C · U · T · L · I · S · T

REAR BOX

FRONT AND BACK PANELS .. 2 ... ½ IN. × 7¹¹⁄₁₆ IN. × 12⅜ IN.

SIDE PANELS .... 2 ... ½ IN. × 3¾ IN. × 12⅜ IN.

MIDDLE DIVIDER .... 1 ... ½ IN. × 3¼ IN. × 11⅞ IN.

BOTTOM........................ 1 ... ⅝ IN. × 3½ IN. × 7⁷⁄₁₆ IN.

FRONT BOXES

PANELS .... 8 ... ½ IN. × 3¾ IN. × 12⅜ IN.

BOTTOMS .... 2 ... ⅝ IN. × 3½ IN. SQ.

LID

SIDES .... 4 ... ½ IN. × 1¾ IN. × 7¹¹⁄₁₆ IN.

TOP .... 1 ... ⅝ IN. × 7½ IN. SQ.

VENEER FOR
INTERIOR PANELS .... 4 ... ¹⁄₃₂ IN. × 4 IN. × 13 IN.

BANDING

MAKE THESE DIMENSIONS A LITTLE THICKER THAN REQUIRED AND FLUSH THEM UP AFTER ASSEMBLY; LENGTHS ARE ROUNDED UP TO NEAREST FOOT.

⅛ IN. × ⅛ IN. × 14 FT.

⅛ IN. × ¼ IN. × 6 FT.

⅛ IN. × ½ IN. × 7 FT.

LEATHER

¹⁄₁₆-IN. THICKNESS (2 OZ. TO 3 OZ.), APPROX. 8 SQ. FT.

⅛-IN.-THICK SHOULDER STRAP (8 OZ.), APPROX. 4 FT. LONG

A SHOPMADE PLANING BOARD

PLANING THIN MATERIAL can be a little tricky without a proper benchtop appliance. Using standard benchdogs in an end vise will generally flex the thin workpiece, and you're bound to hit the benchdogs with your handplane. As an alternative, make a simple planing board to accommodate the task using a piece of stock slightly longer than your longest veneer.

Use some glue and small finish nails to attach ⅛-in.-thick strips, about 1½ in. wide along the back edge and one end of the planing board. This planing jig can be dogged down to your benchtop, and the two thin fences will keep your veneers in place while you plane. Make sure you countersink the nails! If you have any high-friction tape on hand, you could run a few strips down the face of the jig to help keep the veneer in place while you're planing it to final thickness.

A shopmade planing board makes it much easier to plane thin stock.

PREPARING THE STOCK

You have a few options when it comes to making the ½-in.-thick panels for this box. Solid wood would be the first option, but pretty much every time I've used solid wood for small pieces like this one, I've run into wood movement issues. If you have some old, extremely stable stock, you could use it, but the danger of warping and twisting plus veneering to solid wood could still cause difficulties. A second option would be to make a solid-core substrate, as described in the Gentleman's Valet chapter (see p. 166). That project uses a solid-wood core, but because it's prepared and glued in strips you don't have the solid-wood movement concerns.

Another choice would be to use store-bought plywood. It's stable and easily obtainable but I personally don't enjoy working with it for a few reasons; first, it's made with formaldehyde, which concerns me from an environmental standpoint, and second, it isn't very friendly to work with hand tools. You have only the manufacturer's choices of thickness, although you may find some ⅜-in. plywood and can glue the ⅛-in. veneer to it to get the ½-in. thickness we're after.

The option I chose was to create my own shopmade "plywood" using resawn ⅛-in. sheets of holly and three layers of ⅛-in. poplar. The process of resawing by hand is easy and accurate with the kerfing plane and frame saw combination. I began with a holly board about 1 in. thick by 4½ in. wide by 40 in. long. After dimensioning the stock square, set the kerfing plane fence so the cut will be about ³⁄₁₆ in. Saw

> After you cut each veneer, flatten the freshly sawn face of the remaining stock before kerfing in the next cut. This is easier to do while the stock is still thick, and you'll only have one side of the veneer to dress when complete.
>
> TIP

the kerf around the perimeter of the board and resaw this first veneer using the frame saw.

After the two edges are kerfed, make the two cuts across the end grain. The frame saw will drop into this end-grain kerf to start you sawing exactly where you want, and the kerfs down the two outside edges will guide the frame saw down the board.

If you make your own plywood, make sure to cross-band each layer to keep it stable. I purchase the poplar sheets from my local mill. It's extremely inexpensive, and I use it all the time for making templates, shopmade plywood, and any lamination work I have on the go. The poplar is easy to cut with a veneer saw, and I press the panels using liquid hide glue and my veneer press (see p. 196). Whatever option you decide to use, make up the ½-in. panels next.

MAKING THE BOXES

When you have your ½-in. panels made, dimension them to 3¾ in. wide and 12⅜ in. high.

You'll need eight panels for the two front boxes and two panels for the sides of the larger back box. The panel sizes and the rabbet joinery will fit together in such a way to allow an ⅛-in.-sq. void on the outside corners. This space will be filled by a banding later in the project.

Each box has the same joinery: The side panel rabbets are ⅜ in. deep and ¼ in. wide, and the front and back panels get rabbets ⅛ in. deep and ⅜ in. wide. Refer to "Medicine Chest" on p. 142 to see how they fit together. All of the panels receive rabbets across the inside bottoms as well, which allows the bottom of the boxes to nest inside for a stronger glue joint. The bottom rabbets are ⅜ in. deep and ¼ in. wide. The bottom stock is ⅝ in. thick and when inserted into the opening will leave ¼ in. proud at the bottom. This bottom panel will be veneered with walnut and the edges will be covered with banding after the boxes are glued.

When you have the rabbets all cut, dry-fit the two front boxes and make the bottom stock. The bottoms for the two front boxes are

I get four ³⁄₁₆-in. veneers out of the 1-in. board using this method of resawing. It is also a great way to break down thick material for cabinet parts.

1. Rabbet the side panels on the sides ... 2. and on the bottoms. The box bottoms will nest in these rabbets.
3. Detail of corner rabbet joint. The outside corner gap will be filled with ⅛-in. banding after the boxes are glued.

3½ in. sq. and finished at ⅝ in. thick. (I made mine out of some reclaimed softwood that was straight grained and 100 years old; in other words, stable!) Once you've made the bottoms, apply a bottom veneer of walnut. I used the same 1/32-in. walnut veneer I'll use for the inside panel faces.

Make the double-wide panels for the main rear box next. They both receive banding up the center to follow the same outside-corner banding pattern of the front boxes. When the two front boxes are closed, the ⅛-in. banding will look like ¼ in. so the larger panels should match. The inside faces will also be veneered with walnut. This happens

now, before the fretsaw work begins (see the top photo on p. 148).

If you're making your own shopmade plywood, when you make up the larger panels for the front and back of the rear box, sandwich the ¼-in.-wide by ⅛-in. strip of walnut banding on the outside faces of each panel as you go. This will save you from cutting a groove after the panel is made. To begin, I jointed the two back holly panels and glued the walnut banding between them. Once the glue cured, I glued this layer onto three more sheets of ⅛-in. poplar to make up the rear box panel.

SHOPMADE BANDING

CREATING YOUR OWN shopmade banding is easy and enjoyable with the kerfing plane and frame saw. The key to good-looking banding, especially when it will flank store-bought veneer, is careful stock selection. Try to find a piece of solid stock that is straight grained and as close to the same tone and grain structure as the veneer you'll be using. When you make the bandings, saw them a little wider and thicker than needed, which will allow you to plane them flush after they're applied to the piece.

1. Using the same process as for shop-sawn veneer, begin by sawing a kerf at the width of the banding you'll be making. For this project, we'll need both ⅛-in. and ¼-in. stock. Make these a little heavy so you can plane them flush later. Once the kerf is made around the perimeter of the plank, saw the strips out with the frame saw. 2. The planing board comes in handy while working this thin material. 3. After the stock is dressed, set the kerfing plane fence to the desired width and rip out your banding. The kerfing plane is ideal for ripping thin strips from thin stock. (This is a task generally suited for a tablesaw and an operation not usually used in a hand tool–only woodshop.)

Veneer the inside panels using hot hide glue.

SAWING THE WINDOWS

With the panels made and veneered and the banding all ready to go, you're ready for the next step: cutting out the "windows" on the inside panels. This is an optional feature, but one that I chose to add for reasons of aesthetics and utility: For a wine tote, it's nice to be able to see the vintners' labels without having to remove the bottles beforehand. With that in mind, decide on a shape for your windows and use a simple bird's-mouth appliance and a fretsaw to cut out the shape. My bird's mouth is nothing more than two offcuts glued and screwed together, with the table portion having a V notched out.

To begin the window cutout, I first made a template and scribed the shape onto the panels (see "Window Pattern" on p. 142). I determine the radius of the curved areas and drill holes to match. These make the sawing easier because I won't have to freehand the curves with my saw, and they allow an entry point to begin fretsawing.

If you've never done any fretsaw work, spend a morning and practice. It really isn't difficult once you get used to the motion. Hold the fretsaw horizontally and use an up-and-down stroke. One hand holds and pivots the workpiece while you saw with the other (see photo 3 on the facing page). The trick is to keep the sawblade relatively stationary and instead move the workpiece around as you saw.

Glue the walnut banding between the back holly veneers before the ½-in. panel is made. This saves having to cut a groove afterward.

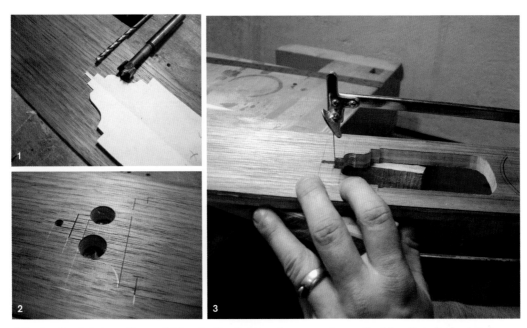

1. Begin with a full-size pattern and determine the diameter of any curved areas. For this pattern, the top hole is $^5/_{32}$ in. and the inside of the elongated S curve, or *cyma recta*, uses a $^1/_2$-in. bit. 2. Scribe the profile and drill the entry holes. 3. A fretsaw with a long throat will make it easier to execute this pattern. The blade I'm using here is a 5-in. double-skip-tooth, 2/0 blade.

Once you get the windows sawn on all four of the inside panels, clean up the sawcuts with some file work and then give them a sealer coat of dewaxed, super-blond shellac. The shellac will protect the windows in the next step. (If you used solid wood for these panels you can omit this stage.) Cover the faces of the windows with clear packing tape (so no stain gets on the outside faces of the panels), and working with an artist's brush from the inside of the panels, apply an ebony stain to the inside edges. This will create a less noticeable transition between the walnut veneer faces and the interior leather.

The next step is to cut a groove on the inside of the two wide panels, using 6-in. extension rods to extend the reach of a small plow plane. This groove will house a $^1/_4$-in.-thick tongue cut into the middle divider. Cut the matching tongue in the middle divider now and dry-fit the box.

APPLYING THE LEATHER

With the panels and joinery complete for the three main boxes, it's time to work some leather. (Note that this step is optional: If you

1. Working from the inside of the panels, apply ebony stain to the inside edges. This will make the transition from the walnut veneer to the inside of the boxes look a little cleaner. 2. Window panels complete after ebony stain has been applied to the inside edges.

1. Use a straightedge and sharp knife to cut out the leather panels. 2. Apply the leather to the panels using hot hide glue. I made up a few at a time using the veneer press. 3. The leather lining on the side panel should finish short of the bottom of the panels so it doesn't interfere with the joinery. 4. Trimming the fat off one of the bottom panels after the glue is dry.

decide not to line the inside of the boxes, then move along to the glue-up after you clean up all the box parts.)

Working with leather makes a nice change of pace and is easy and enjoyable. Think of it as a soft veneer and treat it as such. A straightedge and a sharp knife are essential. The leather for the lining should be no more than 1/16 in. thick; that's 2 oz. to 3 oz. by weight. You have to fit

the leather carefully so it doesn't interfere with the joinery, which means the leather has to be cut so it almost has "built-in" rabbet joints. For example, the bottom of the side panels needs to stop short of the bottom leather panel or the joint will never close properly. You can use hot hide glue to quickly attach the leather to the wood. Measure, mark, and cut out the leather for the interior of the boxes. I left the leather

CUTTING AROUND THE WINDOWS

THE WINDOWS REQUIRE a bit of a trick when lining the inside of these panels. Cut the leather panel to size and lay it face down with the window panel on top. Make sure to line it up with the inside edges of the rabbets and, working from the front, mark the outline of the windows with a felt-tip pen. Remove the window panel and cut out the shape in the leather.

1. Mark the window openings on the backside of the leather panels with a felt-tip pen. 2. Use a leather punch to establish the round at the top of the window profile. The rest is easily cut with chisels. 3. It's a good idea to make the window cutouts in the leather lining slightly oversize so you don't see the leather edging from the front.

about 1/16 in. oversize and trimmed it after the glue was cured.

With all of the leather lining complete, dry-fit the boxes. A few elastic bands are great for keeping things in place while you check the final fit before glue (see the photo below).

GLUING THE BOXES

Now you're ready to clean up the panels and glue the boxes. Start with the two front boxes and move on to the larger rear box. Gluing the back box is the same process as the two front boxes, except that when you have the sides and bottom in place you need to apply some glue to the middle divider tongue and

The glue-up: What's that expression? You can never have too many clamps!

The dry-fit is an important step. It gives you time to notice any small errors before you commit to glue.

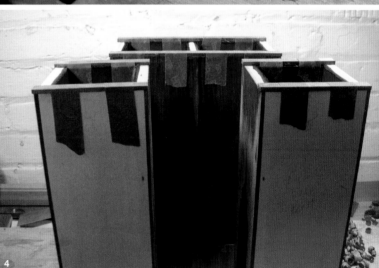

1. Measure the banding. Making these a little oversize will allow you to trim them to fit after the glue has cured. Cut a slight bevel along the inside edges to help them seat better in the corners. 2. Painter's tape is enough to hold the banding tight while the hot glue cures. 3. Plane the banding flush after the glue sets. 4. Cut the top banding and trim to fit once the glue has cured. Apply the two full-length edges first and then carefully fit the middle sections between. Sneak up on a perfect fit with a shooting board, taking light passes until the pieces fit in snug.

slide it down into the grooves inside the back box. This makes up the middle divider in the rear box.

APPLYING THE BANDING

Once the glue has cured you can apply banding to the boxes. Starting with the sides, measure and cut the pieces to fit. Use hot hide glue and painter's tape to hold the bandings in place while the glue sets up. Plane the banding flush after the glue is set. (This is the nice thing about making your own banding a little thicker than required.)

Finish by cutting and applying the top and bottom banding. These pieces can be mitered to give the piece a more traditional look or left as simple butt joints for a more contemporary feel (my preference).

MAKING THE LID

With the four boxes banded, move onto the lid. When I made up my main box stock, I made the "plywood" long enough to get the lid sections out of the same pieces. I marked the pieces and kept them in order for grain continuity between the sides and the lid panels. The joinery for the top is exactly the same as it was for the sides. The side panels of the box top get rabbets $\frac{3}{8}$ in. deep by $\frac{1}{8}$ in. wide, while the front and back rabbets are $\frac{1}{4}$ in. deep and $\frac{3}{8}$ in. wide. The top inside of the lid panels will also receive a $\frac{1}{4}$-in.-wide by $\frac{3}{8}$-in.-deep rabbet. This is the same process we used for the bottom. The lid will nest inside this opening, making for a stronger assembly.

Next make the lid for the top of the box. The lid is dimensioned to $\frac{5}{8}$ in. thick and should finish at $7\frac{1}{2}$ in. sq. Cut the $\frac{1}{8}$-in. holly and

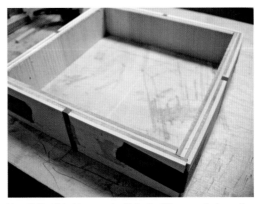

Dry-fit the lid side panels. Note that the panels have the banding inlaid, which is a benefit of making your own shopmade plywood.

walnut banding for the top of the lid. I found it easier to make the top veneer in two sections before applying it to the lid stock. I cut the four holly squares and the crosspieces of walnut

After the lid is veneered, trim the edges flush on the shooting board and dry-fit the lid to the top.

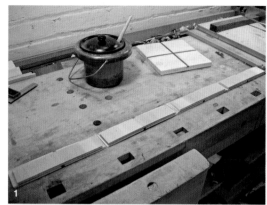

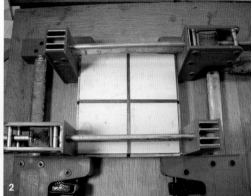

1. Lay the lid sides face down in sequence on the benchtop with painter's tape stretched across the front corners. Apply the glue, fold the assembly together, and press the lid into place. 2. Clamps on the corners draw everything in tight while the glue cures. 3. Plane the banding flush with the lid. Running the top banding grain direction clockwise around the perimeter will make planing easier.

banding, and glued the two halves separately before applying the entire top panel to the lid. Glue the top veneers to the lid core and place in the veneer press to cure. I made mine a little oversize and trimmed them flush to the lid sides on the shooting board.

Now glue up the lid. Place the four sides in sequence, face down on your bench with painter's tape across the front of the corners. Apply the hot glue to the rabbets from the back and fold the box together. Once everything is square, quickly apply glue to the inside rabbets on the top and press the lid into place. This will

hold the top square while the glue sets up. Four clamps on the corners will draw the lid tight into square around the top.

With the lid lined with leather, apply the bottom banding on the lid. Leave the ends long and flush them up when the glue sets.

After the glue sets, remove the clamps and apply the side and top banding on the lid. This is the same process as for the side boxes earlier. Glue the 1/8-in. side banding first and then trim it to fit before applying the top banding. Leave the bottom banding off for now; it will be applied after the interior of the lid is lined with leather. When the top banding is set, plane everything flush with a block plane.

After the lid is banded, line the inside with leather. This is much easier than fitting the bottom boxes earlier. Glue the inside top first, followed by the two opposite sides. Once dry, the final two ends will finish the job.

Now you can attach the bottom banding, which can be made a little proud of 1/2 in. to cover the bottom edge of the leather for a clean and finished look. It's applied in the same sequence as for the lower boxes: front and back edges first and then the two sides fit between them for a tight fit. Leave the ends long and flush them up when the glue sets.

INSTALLING THE HARDWARE

With the lid complete, go over all of the boxes with a card scraper to clean them up. Apply a couple of coats of shellac now before

A flush-cutting saw is handy for removing the ends of the banding. Follow up with a block plane.

1. Scribe the perimeter of the hinge mortises.
2. Set a marking gauge using the leaf of the hinge for an accurate mortise depth. 3. Make a series of chisel cuts along the area to remove. This is one of the front box sides. 4. Carefully remove the waste with a router plane. You can do this freehand with a chisel, but I'm able to get a more consistent depth using the router plane. 5. Test the fit. Slightly shallow? Cut away a little more material. Too deep? Add a thin shim of veneer until the depth is just right.

1. Center the quadrant hinge on the side wall of the box. Fold the top hinge leaf over the back of the box to determine the distance of the mortise. The barrel needs to be outside the back edge for the hinge to operate properly. 2. After scribing the area to mortise, drill two $5/16$-in. holes to the proper depth to establish the round ends of the hinges. 3. After some chisel work, use a small router plane to refine the depth of the hinge mortise. The small router is easier to balance on the thin edges of these side walls. 4. Detail of hinge mortise. Test the fit and predrill the screw holes.

the hardware goes on. (The seal coat of shellac will protect the boxes while you work on the hardware.) For the hardware, you'll need two sets of box hinges for the front boxes, one set of quadrant hinges for the lid, and two lock sets to hold it all together.

INSTALLING THE BOX HINGES

Begin with the box hinges on the sides of the main box (see the photos on p. 157). Carefully

H A R D W A R E

AVAILABLE FROM LEE VALLEY TOOLS

2 SETS OF BRUSSO® $5/16$-IN. × $1\frac{1}{4}$-IN. BOX HINGES (ITEM #01B0302)

1 SET OF BRUSSO $5/16$-IN. × 1-IN. QUADRANT HINGES (ITEM #01B0501)

2 VIOLA BOX LOCKS (ITEM #00F10.07)

TO ATTACH LOCK SETS: 1 PKG. #1 × $3/8$-IN. FLATBRASS SCREWS (ITEM #91Z0102)

BRASS RIVETS: $1/2$ IN. TO $5/8$ IN. (ITEM #33K62.03)

measure and scribe the area where they need to be mortised. Set the depth of a marking gauge using the leaf of the hinges. Begin with light chisel cuts and remove the waste with a small router plane or some more chisel work. For these hinges to function properly, the square barrel has to be outside of the box edges. Take that into account when you're laying out the mortise.

Repeat this process for all four hinge locations. Use a center punch to locate the screw holes and drill them next. If you have matching stainless-steel screws, drive them in first to establish the thread; if not, say a prayer and rub a bit of wax on the brass screws that came with the hinges! These are notorious for breaking, so tread lightly.

INSTALLING THE QUADRANT HINGES

Now move on to the quadrant hinges for the lid. These can be pretty intimidating if you've never installed them before, but there isn't too

Use an ⅛-in. brad-point bit to drill away the bulk of the waste for the stay mortises and then refine with a small chisel.

much to worry about if you're careful with laying out the locations before beginning. Easier said than done!

Begin by scribing the hinge locations and the perimeter of the area to mortise. Lay the hinge on the back edge of the box with the top

Test the fit after the stay mortises are cut. These are deeper than needed, but I prefer knowing they're not going to cause problems later if they're too shallow.

1. Place the lock in the desired location, centered on the side wall of the chest and mark the screw locations. Scribe the perimeter and drill the ends with a 5/16-in. Forstner bit. 2. Selvedge mortise complete. Apply painter's tape to the front of the chest and mark the width of the mortise for the body of the lock. 3. Remove the bulk of the waste with a 1/4-in. brad-point bit. The blue painter's tape serves as a depth gauge. 4. Use a chisel to square the ends. 5. Test-fit the locks in the mortises.

leaf hanging over the back. This will determine the distance needed from the back of the box. Center the hinges on the sides of the box walls. Again, set a marking gauge for the depth using the leaf of the hinge as a guide. Mark the screw-hole locations, and using a ⁵⁄₁₆-in. Forstner bit, drill the front and back round portions out first. Follow with some chisel work and a router plane to establish the depth. Slowly work and test the fit as you go until you have a good-fitting hinge mortise. Repeat on the other side.

With the mortises complete in the top of the rear box, clamp the lid onto the back of the box and transfer the location of the hinge mortises. Use the same method to cut the lid mortises next.

After you have the hinges mortised and are happy with the fit, press the hinges into position and mark the area for the stays—the side-arm stops that control the lid's travel. The stays determine how far the lid opens and need to slide into mortises in the top and bottom box parts when the lid is closed. With the hinges in place, mark the location of the stay mortises. Remove the hinges and drill out the waste. Refine the mortise with a chisel and test-fit the hinge with the stays in place (see the photos on p. 159). These mortises can be made deeper

than necessary to alleviate the risk of the stay bottoming out when the lid is closed. Both sides of the hinge location receive these mortises.

INSTALLING THE LOCKS

The locks aren't completely necessary for the box to function. You could use a catch or clasp to hold the front boxes in place, but I think the locks add a fine element and elevate the design overall. If you add locks, finding small ones suitable for this case may be difficult. The ones I'm using here are sold at Lee Valley and are a perfect fit for the ½-in. thickness of the chest walls.

Begin by placing the lock upside down, centered on the edge of the front wall (see photo 1 on the facing page). I offset the locks toward the middle of the case but this isn't critical: It depends on where you'd like the keyholes to fall visually on the front of the chest. When you're happy with the location, scribe the perimeter of the selvedge and mark the screw-hole locations. Coincidentally, the round portion of these locks is the same ⁵⁄₁₆-in. dia. as the quadrant hinges we just installed. Using the same Forstner bit, drill the outside edges of the selvedge mortise and chisel away the waste between. Test-fit the depth and when all is well,

1. Measure the keyhole locations on the front of the boxes and then drill the barrel portion of the hole. 2. Use the brass plate that comes with the lock as a template to mark out the bottom of the keyhole and then chisel away the waste.

mark the main mortise for the body of the lock. This area is mortised using a ¼-in. brad-point bit to remove the bulk of the waste, following up with a chisel to refine the perimeter.

Once you're happy with the lock locations, drill some pilot holes for the screws and measure and mark for the keyhole (see photo 1 on p. 161). Make a sacrificial block to fill the body mortise before drilling the keyholes. This will prevent the thin walls of the chest from blowing out inside the mortise. With the two barrel portions of the keyholes drilled, use the brass plate that comes with the lock as a template to mark out the bottom of the keyhole. Chisel away the waste, keeping the filler block in place inside the mortise to prevent any damage.

Once the body of the lock fits well inside the mortise and the keyholes are to your liking,

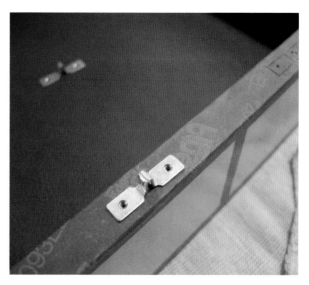

With the catch stuck to the bottom of the lid with double-sided tape, trace the profile onto the painter's tape to locate the position of the mortises.

Land of the giants? This miniature router plane made by Veritas is a 3-in. replica of its full-size counterpart. The blade is only ⅛ in. wide, making it the perfect fit for removing the waste in this tiny mortise.

Locate and mark the pin holes for the brass plates. I applied a small bit of ebony stain to the inside of the keyholes, which makes for a cleaner looking transition.

insert the catches into the locks and apply small tabs of double-sided tape to the top of them to hold them in place. Put some painter's tape on the edge of the lid and close it down tightly in place on the locks. When you reopen the lid, the catches will be stuck in the proper place on the lid and you'll be able to mark the screw locations and scribe around the perimeter of the catches through the painter's tape. When complete, remove the catches and the tape and cut the shallow mortises in the edge of the lid.

Finish off the catch mortises and test-fit the lock assembly. If everything looks good, remove the hardware and get set up for the final finish.

FINISHING AND FINAL DETAILS

I used a dewaxed super-blond shellac on my medicine chest. If you think you'll be using yours outdoors, you might want to consider a top coat. I've heard many arguments about putting polyurethane over shellac, especially waxed shellac. I personally never had issues with a top coat of poly over dewaxed shellac, but if this is something that concerns you,

finish the chest with whatever product you'd like. I used the shellac with only a top coat of wax. I'm careful to apply shellac with an artist's brush on the inside edges of the window cutouts as well as on all of the edges and faces. Apply the shellac in light coats using a 2-lb. cut, sanding lightly between coats.

When you're happy with the finish, reinstall the hardware. This is the time to wax those brass screws before sinking them. Give the interior leather a good rub of beeswax to freshen it up and apply the lock plates. I used the old garlic trick on the brass plate before gluing and installing them (see p. 111). You'll need some tiny pins for these plates as well. I had some in my tool cabinet but needed to cut them down in length. The placement of the lock inside the 1/2-in. walls of the chest dictates that the pins can be no longer than 3/16 in. at most. Predrill the plate holes and use a small amount of hide glue to install the brass keyhole plates. Finish by nailing brass furniture tacks to the bottom outside corners; the tacks make perfect feet for small chests like this one.

One final optional detail is to add a shoulder strap, as explained in the sidebar on p. 164.

ADDING A SHOULDER STRAP

BECAUSE THIS CHEST is used as a wine tote, it needs to be transportable. I purchased a heavy belt strap that matched the thin leather lining. The strap is square at its ends so I began by rounding the ends. Then I punched a series of holes through the leather to accommodate the brass rivets that attach it to the walls of the chest. I arranged seven rivets to give the strap an industrial-modern feel. You can decide on what works best for your own style, but if you'll be transporting four bottles of liquid, make sure the strap is strong enough to hold the weight. (Note: If you're making this as a jewelry box or some other stay-at-home decorative chest, there isn't any need for a shoulder strap.)

Once the holes are punched in the leather, transfer the locations to the back portion of the chest sides. Locate the holes and drill. I used a dimensioned block placed inside the opening to prevent blowout on the interior of the chest. The rivets I used are suitable for material thicknesses from $\frac{1}{2}$ in. up to $\frac{5}{8}$ in.

Install the rivets from the inside out. Push them out through the side holes and reinstall the blocking material. Place the leather strap on the outside over the protruding rivets and nail the rivets together.

1. Punch the holes in the leather strap for the brass rivets. 2. Drill the matching holes in the chest sides. The block inside the chest helps prevent any blowout on the inside of the chest sides while drilling. 3. Insert the female ends of the rivets from the inside of the chest walls. 4. Place the leather strap over the rivets and drive the male ends home.

THE
GENTLEMAN'S
VALET

"Fashions fade,
style is eternal."

—Yves Saint-Laurent

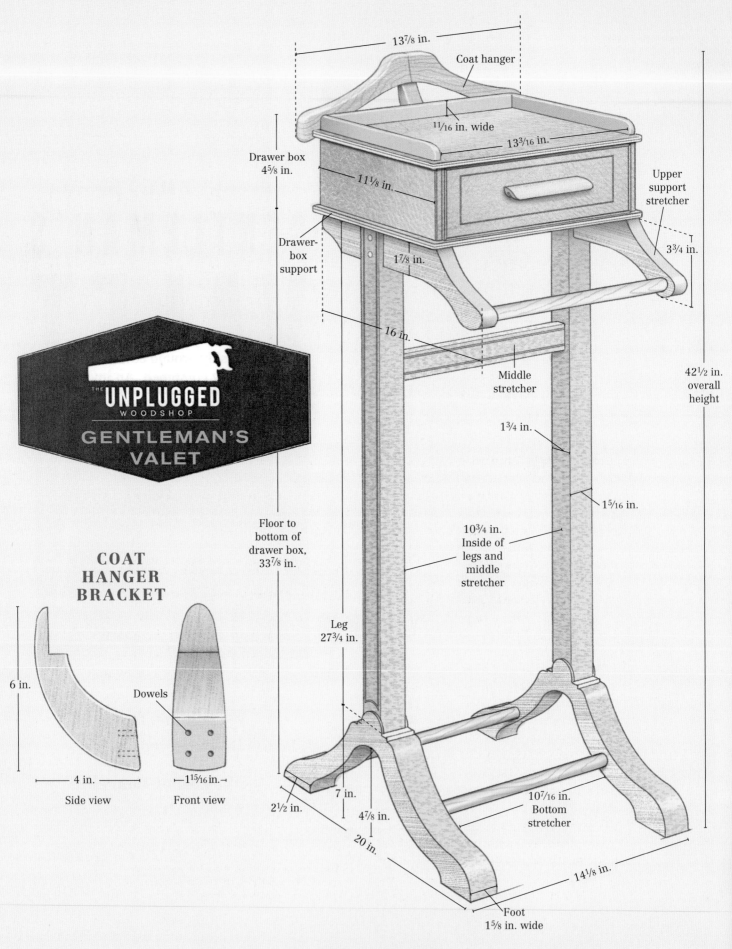

13⁷⁄₈ in.

Coat hanger

¹¹⁄₁₆ in. wide

13³⁄₁₆ in.

Drawer box
4⁵⁄₈ in.

11⅛ in.

Upper
support
stretcher

3¾ in.

Drawer-
box
support

1⅞ in.

16 in.

Middle
stretcher

42½ in.
overall
height

1¾ in.

1⁵⁄₁₆ in.

10¾ in.
Inside of
legs and
middle
stretcher

Floor to
bottom of
drawer box,
33⅞ in.

Leg
27¾ in.

COAT
HANGER
BRACKET

6 in.

Dowels

4 in.

1¹⁵⁄₁₆ in.

Side view

Front view

2½ in.

7 in.

4⁷⁄₈ in.

20 in.

10⁷⁄₁₆ in.
Bottom
stretcher

14⅛ in.

Foot
1⁵⁄₈ in. wide

THE UNPLUGGED
WOODSHOP

GENTLEMAN'S
VALET

DATING BACK TO the mid-1500s, the word *valet* originally referred to a personal manservant responsible for taking care of a gentleman's clothes, appearance, and manners. It may also refer to a wooden stand designed to hang clothing with added utility for shoes, wallet, watch, and jewelry. The modern gentleman, who may take fashion seriously, will appreciate having a valet stand on hand to keep quality garments wrinkle-free when getting prepared for the morning fuss the night before.

The design for this valet, which is relatively small, offers an array of hand-tool techniques that will sharpen your skills as well as open the door to some basic veneering techniques. A project like this is somewhere to express your personal style by adding visual embellishments and ornamentation. Let your imagination soar!

The drawer-box section is made of shop-made solid-core substrate. The construction is mitered joints and splines, a deceptively strong joinery method that will stay put for decades of daily use. With any project that has only a few components, it's a good idea to use your finest stock. Making a mitered box involves an appli-ance known as a miter shooting board that you may or may not be familiar with (see p. 178). We'll also make a veneer press for laying up the panels with some shopmade "plywood" for the rear panel (see p. 196).

MAKING FULL-SIZE DRAWINGS

Whenever I build a piece of furniture that has curved elements or elaborate shapes such as this piece, I take the time to draw full-size templates. The templates eliminate the guess-

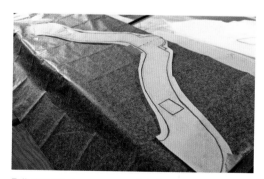

Full-size drawings are essential when working with irregular-shaped components. Use carbon paper to transfer the shapes onto the stock.

FOOT

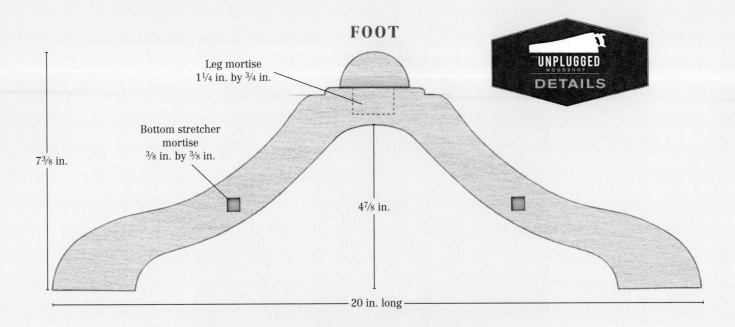

Leg mortise
1¼ in. by ¾ in.

Bottom stretcher
mortise
⅜ in. by ⅜ in.

7⅜ in.

4⅞ in.

20 in. long

DRAWER-BOX SUPPORT

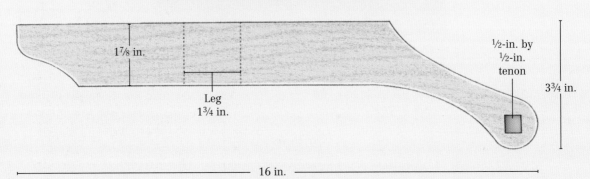

1⅞ in.

Leg
1¾ in.

½-in. by
½-in.
tenon

3¾ in.

16 in.

COAT HANGER
(FRONT VIEW)

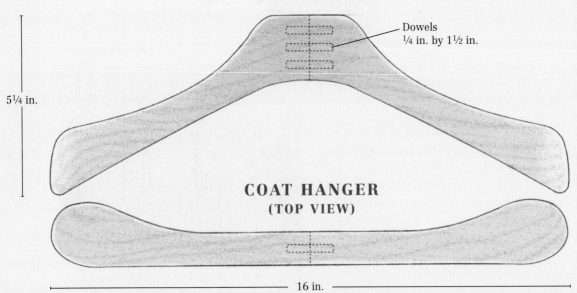

Dowels
¼ in. by 1½ in.

5¼ in.

COAT HANGER
(TOP VIEW)

16 in.

work and make the layout less stressful. I use inexpensive parchment paper from my local grocery store for the patterns and then, with carbon paper, carefully trace them onto my stock.

The feet, coat hanger, and brackets are ready for rough sawing.

SHAPING THE CURVED PARTS

The valet design has a few components with curves, and my method is basically the same for each part. I draw the full-size pattern and then trace them using the carbon paper (if you plan on making more than one valet, ⅛-in. wooden templates would be beneficial to produce). The parts are roughsawn with a bowsaw and the shapes are refined with rasps, spokeshaves, and files. After I get all of the curved parts of the project roughed out, I move onto the legs and cross-members and saw them out as well. All of the parts are planed, squared (where applicable), and smoothed.

When the feet are smooth, move on to shaping the parts for the coat hanger. The hanger is made from two pieces joined in the middle and doweled together (see "Coat Hanger" on facing page), which gives a nice book-matched appearance to the hanger. Dowel centers help locate the mating holes, and once glued, the shape of the hangar is refined. I gave

Use rasps to define the curves after rough sawing.

the hanger a light coat of oil at this stage to see what the book-matched grain will look like with finish.

The hanger sits in a notched bracket that is held with dowels and a screw on the rear panel of the drawer box. Refer to "Coat Hanger Bracket" on p. 168 and rough-saw the shape of the bracket. Refine the curves with hand tools and drill the dowel holes in the bottom of the block. The notch for the hanger is carefully scribed so the two will mate perfectly when glued.

BUILDING THE BASE

After all the curved components are roughsawn and refined using a variety of shaping tools, move on to the legs and cross-members. These are dimensioned and the mortise-and-tenon joints are marked and cut. Special attention

Clamp both feet together and shape them at the same time for both speed and continuity sake. This also works for the drawer-box support arms.

TIP

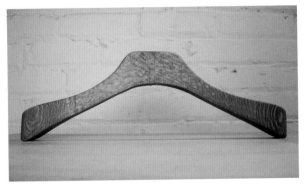

A light coat of oil/varnish on the completed coat hanger brings out the grain.

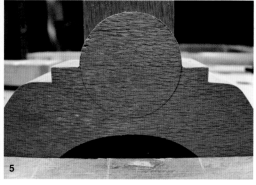

1. Sawkerfs mark the width of the waste area between the cheeks of the foot. **2.** Cut the leg mortise into the top of the foot, being careful not to break the cheeks. **3.** Use dividers to mark the circular profile desired. **4.** Fair the curve with rasps, files, and sandpaper. Notice the blocking between the cheeks. **5.** A dry-fit. This round area would be a nice place to add a decorative element like inlay or carving.

should be given to the mortises in the feet where they meet the legs because they're not as straightforward as they look. The feet have "cheeks" that need to be left attached, and care must be taken not to break them while proceeding through the mortising steps.

To begin, lay out the area that needs to be removed in the top of the foot and saw away the waste. The waste area is 1⁵/₁₆ in. wide by 1¾ in. long by 1 in. deep and should fit the leg bottom snugly. Some blue painter's tape around the "ankles" will give instant feedback

Paper templates assist in locating mortises in curved components (here, the top drawer-box supports).

if you saw too deep. Remove the waste with a bowsaw and then clean up with a chisel. Once the area is clear, mark the mortise location and bore out the waste with a brace and bit. Square the mortise with a chisel and cut and fit the tenons in the leg bottoms.

Shape the cheeks left on the ankles into half circles. Outline the shape with a pair of dividers and then carefully form using a rasp, files, and finally some sandpaper. When forming these half-circle shapes, I use the offcut I removed as blocking to support the thin stock at the ankle.

The bottom cross-stretcher mortises that are required on the inside of the feet, as well as the ones in the top drawer-box supports, all need to be carefully located. This can be a challenge because there are no square edges to refer to when laying them out. Again, using full-size drawings, make paper templates and

transfer the location of the mortises over to the curved parts.

The drawer-box supports are attached to the top of the legs with lap joints. Saw the joints, remove the waste with a bowsaw, and clean up

Rough out the top of the leg joint where the drawer-box supports are attached.

The stretchers complete after rounding.

Applying finish as you work through a project helps you see what the grain is going to look like in the finished piece and offers a bit of protection through the rest of the building process.

TIP

the sawmarks with a chisel. When the lap joint is assembled, dowels will be used across the joint to hold it securely in place.

The two bottom stretchers and the stretcher for the drawer support brackets are rounded over. This could easily be done on a lathe, but I enjoy rounding stock with a block plane. I hold the stretchers in a shopmade jig (see "Elevated Bench Dogs" on p. 40) and carefully round them over. To begin, plane the four corners down to make an octagon. Continue planing down each new corner until you have a 16-sided stretcher and then continue this process until they look and feel round. They don't

have to be perfectly cylindrical but only fair to the eye and touch.

With the three cross-stretchers round and fair, I spend some time cleaning up the base components. I fair the curves and chamfer the edges. The drawer-box supports are shaped and planed until they fit snugly into the tops of the legs. At this point I give a quick coat of oil/varnish to the feet, cross-stretchers, and drawer-box supports.

MAKING THE DRAWER BOX

The drawer-box carcase is a mitered box construction with added splines. The box will be veneered and have moldings applied. I made a

Dry-fit the drawer-box supports.

1. Rip the pieces for the drawer box solid-core substrate from a piece of 8/4 poplar. 2. Apply solid lacewood edging to the front edge of the drawer-box pieces with hot hide glue and then plane the edging flush. 3. The drawer-box panels with edging, ready for the interior veneer.

solid-core substrate to avoid any wood movement issues, but you could also use stable, solid wood or even plywood.

Start by rip-cutting some 2-in. poplar to make up the solid-core substrate. Dimension the stock to $^3/_8$ in. thick and crosscut, joint, and glue the strips together to make up the four panels for the drawer box. I added a $^1/_2$-in. strip of lacewood along the front and back edges of the four panels. The top and bottom panels should finish at $11^3/_{16}$ in. long by $13^3/_{16}$ in. wide by $^3/_8$ in. thick, with the side panels finishing at $11^3/_{16}$ in. long by $3^{15}/_{16}$ in. wide, and again $^3/_8$ in. thick. Having solid material on the front and back of the solid-core substrate allows for beveling and slight chamfers later. If veneer were used on the outside edges, no edge profiles would be possible.

Use hot hide glue to apply the lacewood edging and press in place with a bit of tape to hold it down. Leave the edging a little proud of the finished core thickness and plane flush when the glue is fully cured.

VENEERING THE BOX

The next step is to veneer the inside of the drawer box. I size the veneer about $^1/_8$ in. larger than needed. Joint the pieces (if necessary) and hold them together using veneer tape on the seams. I use liquid hide glue for this interior veneer application. The panels are put in the veneer press (see p. 196) and left to cook overnight, with $^3/_4$-in. plywood and parchment paper placed between each panel to make sure the pieces remain flat and don't stick together while the glue sets.

Plywood packing keeps the veneered panels flat in a veneer press while the glue sets.

When the panels come out of the press, trim the veneer to size and scrape off any excess glue. Next, miter the edges of the drawer-box panels using the miter shooting board (see p. 178). Scribe the inside of the miters with a marking gauge to give you a crisp reference line to plane down to and to protect the edge of the veneer while planning away the waste. Dry-fit the corners as you go. Clean up the veneer with a card scraper and cut the rear rabbet for the rear drawer-box panel; the rabbet is ¼ in. wide and ⁷⁄₁₆ in. deep (the thickness of the back panel).

Now apply a light coat of oil/varnish to the inside of the panels. Allow the finish to dry and then apply a few coats of citrus wax (it's easier to do this now before the box is glued).

GLUING UP THE DRAWER BOX

Gluing a mitered box is relatively easy with careful planning. I place some parchment paper across my workbench and place the panels edge to edge with the miters facing down to begin. Blue painter's tape applied to the outside

1. Miter the edges of the drawer-box panels on the miter shooting board. 2. Finish the inside of the panels before the glue-up begins.

MITER SHOOTING BOARD

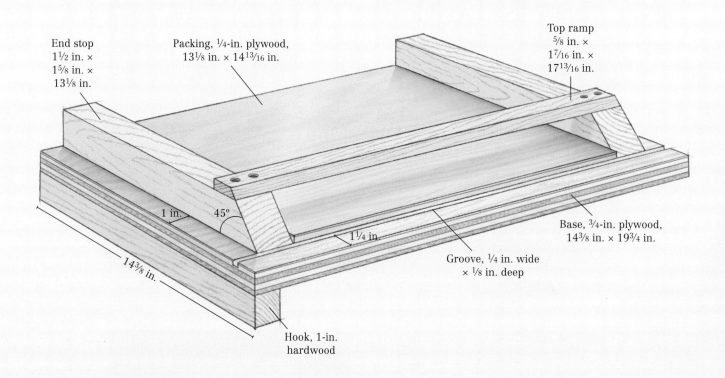

End stop
1½ in. ×
1⅝ in. ×
13⅛ in.

Packing, ¼-in. plywood,
13⅛ in. × 14¹³⁄₁₆ in.

Top ramp
⅝ in. ×
1⁷⁄₁₆ in. ×
17¹³⁄₁₆ in.

1 in.

45°

1¼ in.

14⅜ in.

Groove, ¼ in. wide
× ⅛ in. deep

Base, ¾-in. plywood,
14⅜ in. × 19¾ in.

Hook, 1-in.
hardwood

THE DESIGN for this shooting board originally appeared in an article written by K. G. Wells for *Woodworker Magazine* in 1964. The shooting board has end ramps cut at 45°, making it perfect for tackling long miters using a handplane. The groove in the base and the mitered top ramp allow a handplane

to run across the workpiece held at the desired 45° angle. The workpiece stays flat to the work surface and the handplane is held at the angle.

I use the shooting board for small, mitered boxes (as in the gentleman's valet) and cabinet components. I didn't follow the exact sizes of the original Wells design but used his version both for reference and for inspiration.

MAKING THE BASE

To begin, I dimensioned some ¾-in. cherry plywood for the base and cut a small, shallow groove about 1 in. in from one edge with my plow plane. This groove will serve as a track for the edge of a handplane to ride in. High-quality plywood works well for workbench

appliances as it is stable and less prone to warping and movement through the seasons. I keep an inexpensive panel saw in my shop solely for the purpose of sawing plywood.

CUTTING THE MITERED END STOPS

The end stops are made from 8/4 cherry that is planed down to about 1⅝ in. I crosscut them to width and miter the ends. These 45° miters are critical and should be executed carefully.

I used some ¼-in. plywood for "packing," as Wells described it. This thin layer lifts the workpiece being mitered off the bed and away from the plane blade. The packing plywood will be glued to the main ¾-in. plywood

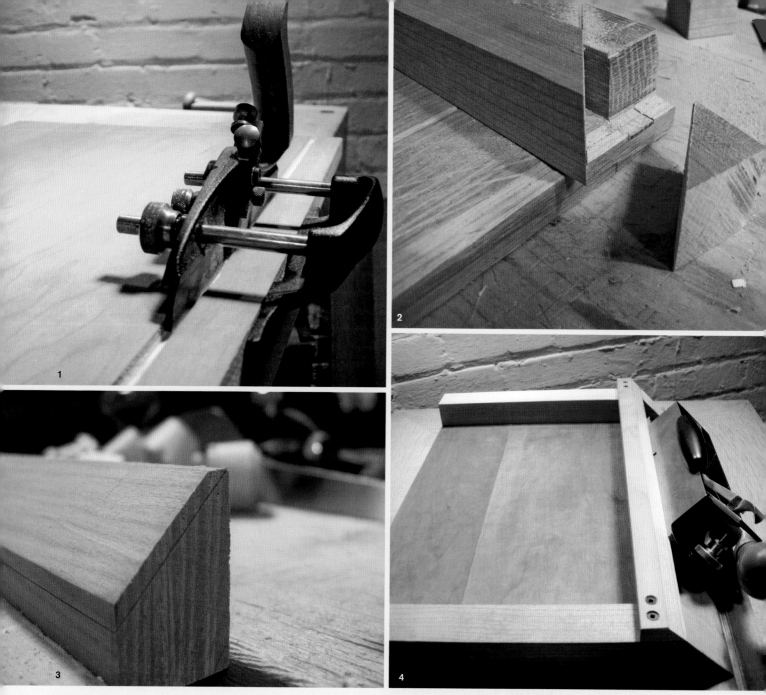

1. Cut a shallow groove into the plywood base using a plow plane. 2. Cut the end stops at 45° and refine the slope with a low-angle block plane.
3. Use a jack plane to remove the bulk of the top ramp material and then follow up with a block plane to refine the angle. 4. Ready to work.

base after it has been carefully fit between the two outside stops.

MAKING THE TOP RAMP

I made the top ramp from 4/4 cherry stock, which is mitered along its length. To begin the miter, use a jack plane to remove the bulk of the material. Fine-tune the angle with a freshly sharpened block plane, be-

ing careful not to plane down past the scribe lines.

With the components complete, glue the end stops and packing plywood in place. Drill screws up through the bottom of the base for added strength in the end stops. Predrill the top ramp and screw it to the top of the end stops.

Make a hook from some scrap wood and glue and screw it to the base. A

quick coat of wax will help keep it clean and keep your plane running smooth. I use a dedicated shooting plane on this appliance but it will work just as well with a jack plane or a jointer. Before you size the thickness of the end stops, just make sure they're the right size for the plane you'll be using.

1. Glue the drawer box and set it aside to dry. A scrap panel pressed into the rear rabbet holds the box square while the glue dries. 2. Cut sawkerfs for hardwood splines along the mitered edges of the drawer box. Glue in some hardwood splines and plane them flush when dry. 3. Fit the drawer front into the front opening; follow with the sides.

of each joint will act like a hinge when the box is assembled. Turn the panels over after the tape is applied and get ready to glue. Once the glue is applied, roll the pieces together to form the box. Precut a scrap piece to the exact size of the rear opening, making sure it's perfectly square. When the panels are folded closed, this scrap panel is pressed into place, ensuring the box will be held square while the glue sets. Wrap tape around the box and set it aside until dry.

Remove the tape and clean up the edges and inside from any glue squeeze-out. Next, prepare the outside corners to receive some hardwood splines. I use my largest backsaw, which has a fairly thick saw plate, and make a series of cuts along the mitered edges. I angle these kerfs much like a dovetail for added strength across the grain. Cut the splines and glue them in place. When the glue is set, remove the waste and clean up the box.

MAKING THE DRAWER

The drawer for this project is a traditional design with half-blind dovetails in the front and through dovetails in the back. The drawer front receives a cock bead and stringing is applied to the face. A custom pull finishes off the drawer.

To begin, saw the solid, lacewood drawer front from 4/4 rough stock. Carefully size the drawer front so it just barely fits into the drawer opening (see photo 3 on the facing page). The drawer sides are made of curly maple and dimensioned to $5/16$ in. thick. These are carefully fit in their locations so they "just" fit as well.

With the front and sides of the drawer fit, scribe the drawer back using the front as a template. The back will be cut down in width so the drawer bottom will slide in underneath it later on. The next step is to cut the drawer bottom groove on the inside of the drawer sides and front. The $1/4$-in. groove is $1/4$ in. up from the drawer bottom and just shy of $1/4$ in. deep. A plow plane makes quick, quiet work of this job.

DOVETAILING THE DRAWER

The first step in cutting the half-blind dovetails on the drawer front is to scribe a line on the drawer front edges that will establish the front lip. I usually make this about $3/16$ in.: any thinner and you run the risk of blowing out the drawer face material; any thicker and you lose that traditional dovetail look we're trying so hard to achieve. Transfer this same measurement around the perimeter on the front of the drawer sides to establish the baseline for the tails.

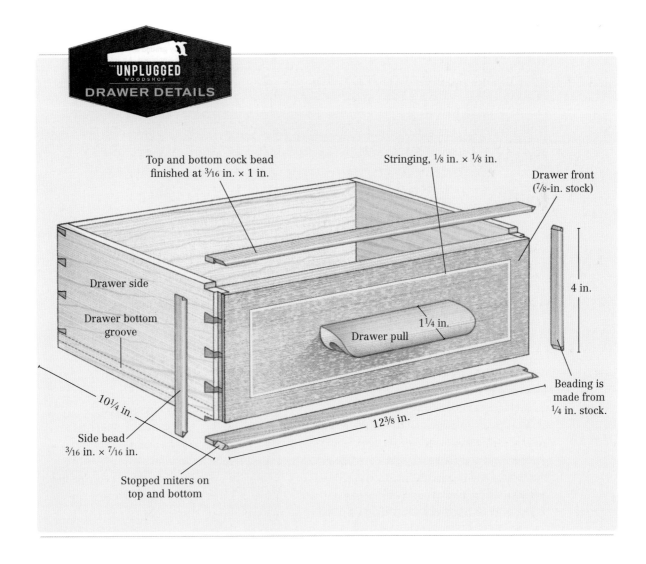

THE UNPLUGGED WOODSHOP
DRAWER DETAILS

Top and bottom cock bead finished at $3/16$ in. × 1 in.

Stringing, $1/8$ in. × $1/8$ in.

Drawer front ($7/8$-in. stock)

Drawer side

Drawer bottom groove

4 in.

$1 1/4$ in.

Drawer pull

Beading is made from $1/4$ in. stock.

$10 1/4$ in.

Side bead $3/16$ in. × $7/16$ in.

Stopped miters on top and bottom

$12 3/8$ in.

1. Scribe the front lip on the drawer front edges. 2. Transfer the measurement to the front of the drawer sides. 3. The lying press is the perfect jig for holding parts while making drawers.

With the depth of the side tails scribed, lay out the dovetails and clearly mark in the waste. Clamp the two drawer sides together in the lying press (see p. 74) and saw them both. Remove most of the waste with a fretsaw and use a chisel to clean up the remainder. With the tails cut, lay each drawer side on the edge of the drawer front and scribe the tails. Carefully saw the sockets and remove the waste with a chisel, as shown in the photos on the facing page.

The drawer back receives through dovetails, which is basically the same treatment. Scribe

There has been much ink spilled over different ways of laying out dovetails: what angle is best, how many tails per inch, should you chisel or fretsaw the waste, and so on. After sawing thousands of dovetails over the years, I've come to realize that these details aren't all that important and shouldn't worry the maker. Even a poorly executed dovetail will be plenty strong, albeit a little less refined aesthetically. Choose whatever method works best for you and proceed.

TIP

1. Use dividers to lay out the tails. 2. Remove most of the waste with a fretsaw. 3. Chisel the remaining waste and clean up the joint. 4. Chop out the waste in the drawer front after the tails have been carefully transferred over from the drawer sides. 5. The top and bottom shoulders are thinner than usual as they will be cut away later when the drawer is beaded. Usually, the dovetails don't go this close to the upper and lower edges of the drawer front because they could easily break.

The through dovetails at the back of the drawer are laid out slightly differently from the front half-blinds. No outside shoulders here.

the base lines on the drawer sides and back and lay out the tails. The rear tails vary in layout. Instead of shoulders on the drawer-side edges, we mark out half-pins. One is just above the drawer-bottom groove and the other about 3/16 in. down from the top of the drawer sides. Look at the photo above showing the layout and study "Details" on p. 181 closely.

Saw and chop out the tails and transfer them over to the drawer back. Saw the pins and remove the waste with a fretsaw and chisel. The drawer back is now ready to be ripped down to final size. Measure the width from the top of the drawer bottom groove to the top of the half-pin cut in the drawer side.

Cut the drawer bottom to size (I used 1/2-in. poplar that finished at 7/16 in. thick after smoothing), making sure the grain runs side to side to allow the bottom to expand and contract. The bottom drawer panel is raised to fit

snugly into the 1/4-in. groove previously cut in the drawer sides and front. When the drawer is assembled, the bottom slides in under the narrow drawer back.

Dovetails complete and ready for glue-up.

1. Plane the drawer sides flush with the front. The high-angle smoothing plane is perfect for dealing with these curly maple drawer parts, and the lying press and a hardwood support block make this process easier. 2. Back corner detail. Notice the half pins at the top and bottom. 3. Use the beading tool to "scratch" the groove for the stringing. 4. Flush up the stringing after the glue sets.

Before gluing the drawer, lightly chamfer all the inside edges of the parts so no sharp corners are left. With that, glue the drawer frame.

When the glue is dry, the lying press comes in handy to flush up the sides and clean up the drawer. Place a scrap of hardwood through the drawer frame with the bottom panel removed so the press holds it in place as you plane. The high-angle smoothing plane is perfect for dealing with the curly maple of the drawer sides. Plane the front maple dovetails carefully until they're just flush with the lacewood drawer front. I try my best not to plane any of the

drawer-front edge because it was sized earlier for that perfect fit.

STRINGING THE DRAWER

The next step in the drawer construction saga is to apply the stringing to the face. This needs to be done before the cock bead is applied because we need the outside edges for referencing the scratch stock when cutting the groove that will house the stringing.

Begin by marking out the location of the stringing and scribe deep, crisp lines in the drawer front. You can get as creative as you

MAKING A SCRATCH STOCK

A SCRATCH STOCK is a dedicated, specialty tool available for cutting grooves for inlay work, but it's easy to make your own. I was able to purchase metal replacement blanks that fit my beading tool and shaped the cutter so the groove is a hair thinner than the stringing. You could easily make your own cutter blanks out of a card scraper or old saw plate. The beading tool is nothing more than a jig to hold the cutter in place. I scribe the width needed for this application and file the blank to size.

1. File a metal blank to the desired size in a metal vise (³⁄₃₂ in. for the holly stringing used on this project). 2. Insert the blank into a beading tool with only the stringing profile protruding.

like with this step: I chose a simple rectangle border.

I used my beading tool to remove the waste in the stringing groove, but first I needed to make and size a cutter to fit the stringing.

The scratch stock easily cuts away the waste, creating the groove. Clean up the corners with a small detail chisel and then miter and carefully fit the stringing. I use a large chisel on my bench hook to cut the miters. Hot hide glue makes quick work of the stringing process, and after a few minutes of drying time, I'm able to scrape and then plane everything flush with the drawer front.

BEADING THE DRAWER

Cock beading gives the drawer a traditional look that complements the overall design and also hides any small gaps or discrepancies around the perimeter of the drawer front. Prepare the beading stock by ripping some 1/4-in. strips of 1-in. lacewood. Leave these pieces longer than you need for now. Use your beading tool to scratch the roundover desired for the bead profile and fine-tune the shape with a block plane.

Set your marking gauge directly off the thickness of the bead stock and scribe deep lines around the perimeter of the drawer front. The drawer top and bottom will be recessed along the entire width and depth of the drawer front, while the sides receive a 3/8-in.-wide rabbet, so the dovetails will still be seen after the bead is applied.

Cut the recess around the perimeter of the drawer front using a skew block plane as well as a shoulder plane. Start with the sides and finish with the full recess on the top and bottom. This order is beneficial in case any material is blown out when planing across the end grain on the sides. Once the top and bottom recess are cut, you'll eliminate any of the blowout. This step demonstrates why I chose to lay out the drawer side dovetails so close to the edges. Once cut away, I still wanted to see a substantial half-tail on the top and bottom. Play around with the

Prepare the beading stock and cut scribe lines around the drawer face.

Cut the recess around the drawer perimeter.

layout until you find something that appeals to you visually.

Cut the top and bottom moldings first; they'll receive a stopped miter because the side pieces are narrower. Saw the miter on a bench hook using a fine jeweler's saw and refine with a sharp chisel. Glue the top and bottom in place and then fit and apply the side pieces.

The stringing and cock beading give the drawer a traditional flair, but I decided to add a more contemporary drawer pull to offset things a little bit and bring this design into the modern era. See the sidebar on p. 190 for directions for making the drawer pull.

HAMMER VENEERING THE DRAWER-BOX EXTERIOR

When we last left the drawer box it had been glued, reinforced with splines, and veneered on the inside only. With the drawer complete, apply the exterior veneer to the drawer box. The process goes like this: Cut the veneer slightly oversize and, if necessary, joint the pieces to make up the width of the drawer box. Tape the joint together on the show side using thin veneer tape, which will be scraped away as soon as the glue sets. The sides are veneered first with the top and bottom to follow. Using hot hide glue is a bit like sprinting; you don't have a heck of a lot of time.

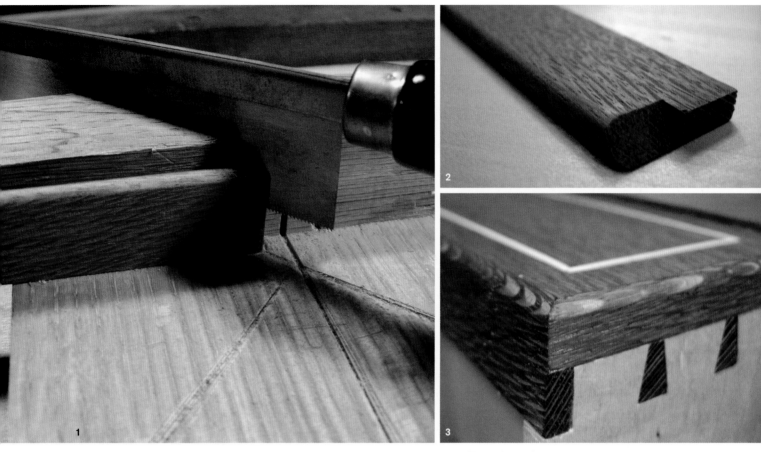

1. Saw stopped miters in the top and bottom moldings. 2. Top molding detail. 3. The cock beading complete.

Place the drawer box on end in your face vise and cover the entire end surface with hot glue. Place the veneer face down in the hot glue and cover the back of the veneer with more hot glue. Work as quickly as you can. Carefully flip the veneer over and, using a veneer hammer like a squeegee, begin in the center and start working the veneer down into the fresh glue. The glue on the veneer face helps lubricate the hammer while you press the veneer into the now cooling glue. Go over the entire surface using moderate to hard pressure, traveling with the grain, and squeeze all of the air out from under the veneer.

In a minute or two you'll start hearing light, crackling sounds that tell you the air is coming out and the glue is beginning to set. Work the surface for another minute until the veneer is securely in place. Before it sets, wipe off the squeeze-out with a damp rag, and when you're confident the veneer is firmly set in place, trim the fat off the edges with either a veneer saw or chisel. The veneer tape can be moistened and is easily removed with a card scraper. Follow

Glue pot, veneer hammer, and finished drawer box. Note the rabbet around the inside perimeter that will hold the back panel.

MAKING A DRAWER PULL

TO BEGIN, I selected a piece of straight-grained holly, which will complement the stringing and make a strong focal point on the drawer front. Saw the stock and plane it square.

Use a molding plane to plane a hollow in the underside of the pull and then turn the piece over and detail the top profile using a block plane. Pencil in the end profiles and take a few sawcuts to remove the bulk of the waste. Refine the curve with a file and use a round card scraper to clean up the inside plane tracks left from the molding plane.

Lightly sand the pull to blend the curves. At this point the tight, white-grained holly looks almost like ivory. Trace the back side of the pull and make a paper template, which is used to locate some holes for attaching the dowels to secure the pull to the drawer front. (A screw will be added from the inside after the pull is glued.)

1. Use a molding plane to establish the hollow. 2. Define the top profile with a block plane. 3. Rough-saw the ends and use a file to blend the curve.

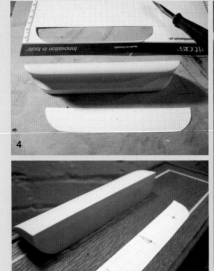 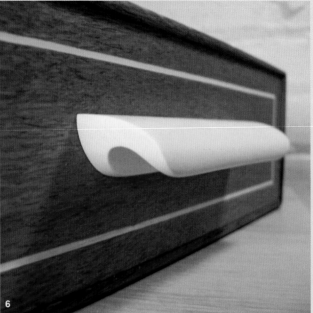

4. Make a paper template to locate the pull on the drawer front. 5. Mark and drill the dowel locations. 6. Complete but only dry-fit. The pull will be permanently fastened after the final finish has been applied.

A close-up view of the edge of shopmade "plywood," before glue-up.

an outer layer of lacewood to begin, then a ⅛-in. layer of poplar running horizontally, a middle layer of ⅛-in. poplar running vertically, and another ⅛-in. of poplar again running horizontally, with a final layer of lacewood veneer to finish. I glue this up using liquid hide glue and set it in the veneer press overnight.

The inside perimeter receives a rabbet to mate with the rabbet already cut on the interior back of the drawer box. When the drawer-box carcase veneer is trimmed and scraped, the plywood panel can be glued into the recess on the drawer-box back.

the same process on the opposite side and then repeat again for the bottom and top. If your edges aren't absolutely perfect, don't sweat it. They'll be covered with moldings in the next stage of construction.

MAKING THE BACK PANEL

The rear drawer-box panel is made from shopmade plywood, which allows me to glue the piece in place without having to worry about wood movement issues, adding both strength and rigidity to the drawer-box construction. I make the plywood from a sandwich of veneer:

MAKING AND INSTALLING MOLDINGS

Moldings applied to the outside edges of the drawer-box top and bottom not only elevate the design but also protect the veneered edges of the box. Select clear, straight-grained 4/4 stock and rip the molding stock to the required thickness of ⅜ in. For now, leave the full 1-in. width, which will give you something to clamp when you shape the profile. I make the edge profile using my trusted beading tool

A special-purpose cutter in a beading tool is used to profile the moldings.

with a formed cutter sized to suit the task (see the bottom photo on p. 191). I work the profile and then rip the molding to its finished width.

Carefully measure the molding to fit and miter the corners. Work your way around the perimeter of the drawer carcase, measuring and cutting as you go in case of slight differences in lengths. When complete and dry-fit, the moldings can be quickly attached using hot hide glue. When the glue has set, round over the outside corners and refine the curves with a file. To finish, touch up the profile using a small needle file and blend the shape with sandpaper.

ADDING THE TOP MOLDINGS

To finish off the solid wood components on this project, rip and dimension some stock to ³/₈ in.

thick and ¹/₂ in. wide for the top edge profile. These pieces are chamfered and then mitered following the same steps as described in the previous molding section. Attach the top edge pieces with ¹/₄-in. dowels. Drill holes in the bottom of the stock and then use dowel centers to locate the corresponding holes to attach the piece to the drawer-box top. When the miters are complete, round over the front ends of the two side pieces.

ATTACHING THE HANGER BRACKET

The coat hanger bracket is attached to the back panel with four ¹/₄-in. wooden dowels 1¹/₄ in. long. Predrill the hanger bracket and insert dowel centers. Press the dowel centers into the back panel to determine the location of the back panel holes. Inside the drawer

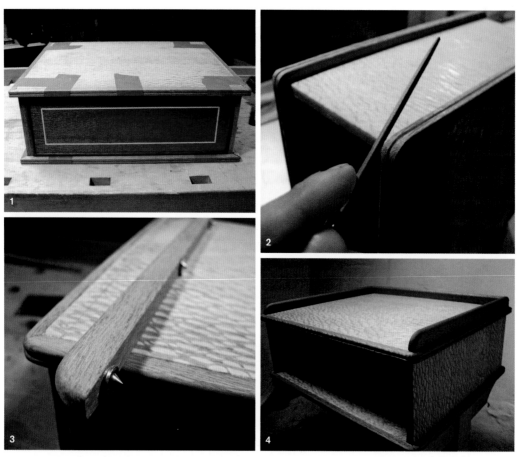

1. Dry-fit the moldings and hold them in place with tape. 2. Round the corners when the glue is dry and use a needle file to redefine the profile that gets cut away during the process. 3. Dowel centers help locate the holes in the drawer-box top. 4. Moldings complete (but still only dry-fit here).

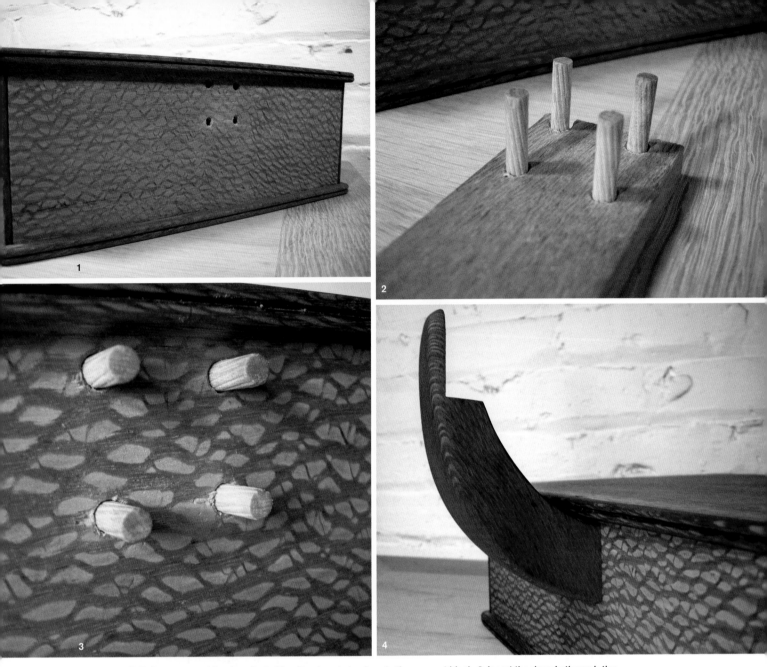

1. Drill the rear panel for dowels. 2. Glue the dowels in place in the support block. 3. Insert the dowels through the rear panel holes. 4. Dry-fit the hanger bracket.

box, a block of scrap wood is also drilled and will be glued in place to reinforce the bond. Drill the holes in the back panel and glue the dowels into the support block. Place the support block inside the drawer box and push the dowels out through the back panel. Attach the hanger bracket. A single screw from the inside out through the block and into the hanger bracket will keep this thing in place for years of use.

DECORATIVE STRINGING AND PREFINISH

With the drawer box complete and the moldings and hanger dry-fit, I add some final details to the piece. Given the style and purpose of the design, I chose to add a few decorative stringing details to complement the drawer front and add a bit of flair to the overall aesthetic of the project. The holly stringing is applied in the same way as for the drawer front—I scribe the groove and, using the same scratch stock I made earlier, carefully remove the material.

The one big difference in this procedure is at the bottom of the legs. I added a half-circle to accentuate the round portion at the top of the feet. You could use a chisel to remove the waste in this section or purchase specialty tools designed to cut recesses specific for radius stringing details (see the sidebar at right).

Monitor the depth of the groove so that, when applied, the stringing will stand slightly proud of the workpiece; it will be planed flush after the glue is fully cured. After you cut the grooves, size the stringing and dry-fit it in place. To bend the rounded portion of the stringing detail at the bottom of the legs, I use an electric kettle fitted with a metal pipe in the spout. As the water comes to a boil the steam heats the pipe and the thin strips of holly are easily bent to shape. Make a few extra pieces as well, you'll no doubt break some while bending . . . I did!

When you have the stringing dry-fit you can start to attach it. Begin by gluing the curved section into the half-round grooves of the leg

TIP Be extremely careful whenever you're using steam to bend wood. A steam burn is one of the worst, so careful preparation and safety should be priorities.

Insert the bottom curved section of the stringing first, followed by the straight pieces; these are mitered to fit by eye. Plane the stringing flush after the glue is dry.

Shopmade radius tool.

A CUTTER FOR STRINGING

STEVE LATTA, a contributing editor for *Fine Woodworking* magazine, designed a wonderful set of inlay tools a few years ago, which are commercially available through Lie-Nielson® Toolworks in Warren, Maine. I don't do a whole lot of stringing in my work, so I couldn't justify purchasing these specialty tools for just a few projects. I did however purchase the cutter for Steve's radius tool for less than $20. Then, in 10 minutes, using a small scrap of hardwood, I made myself a tool that cuts the radius for the leg detail on the valet. If I were doing stringing on a regular basis, I wouldn't think twice about purchasing the tool set.

bottoms. Leave this curved piece slightly long, and once the glue has set for a minute, trim it to fit with a sharp chisel and then install the straight side pieces. Miter the ends of the straight pieces by eye with a sharp chisel and carefully fit in place. When all of the stringing is applied in the legs and upper crosspiece, use a block plane and card scraper to bring the stringing flush.

These stringing details mark the final steps in the project. One last dry-fit and then you can begin the finishing. Go over all of the parts with a smoothing plane, a card scraper, and sandpaper wherever necessary. Everything should be labeled so when you start the final glue-up you'll know what goes where.

I give all of the parts a coat of oil/varnish and let them dry for a couple of days. I follow this with a couple of coats of shellac. I mix the shellac to a 1-lb. cut and rub it on, giving a light sand with 320-grit paper between coats. Let the parts sit overnight and then move onto the final glue-up in the morning. I use hot hide glue for the joints and add a few dowels through the leg top joinery after gluing.

TIP

Label your parts as you work. It's all too easy to inadvertently mix up parts, which leads to a stressful glue-up. Labels should be kept discreet so none will be seen in the finished piece. Write letters and numbers on tenons and inside corresponding mortises.

Although I titled this chapter a gentleman's valet I must confess that my wife has been using this piece on a daily basis since I built it. She lays her work clothes on it every evening. Regardless of who ends up using yours, it's a fun project to make with lots of hand-tool techniques wrapped up in a small footprint.

Prefinish the parts before the glue-up begins.

VENEER PRESS

A VENEER PRESS is a useful workshop appliance if you plan on doing any amount of veneer work. You can get by with cauls and clamps, but a dedicated press, made with solid joinery will translate into better lay-ups with more predictable results. This design is based on a veneer press shown on the Lee Valley Tools website, where I purchased the press screws.

I made my press to accommodate small to midsize panels, using 2-in. poplar stock. The cross-members are joined to the legs with housed through tenons, which are easy to execute and have the strength desired for the application. This joint needs to be rock solid to withstand the force of the screws while in use.

To begin, assemble the cut list and flatten and square all the parts on four sides.

CUTTING THE LEG AND BASE JOINERY

The legs connect to the base with half-lap joints. Make a ¼-in. notch in both the legs and in the mating areas of the base. Mark the locations of each leg and saw a kerf to establish the side of the joint. Remove the waste with a chisel and refine the depth with a large router plane; follow this same procedure for all four legs.

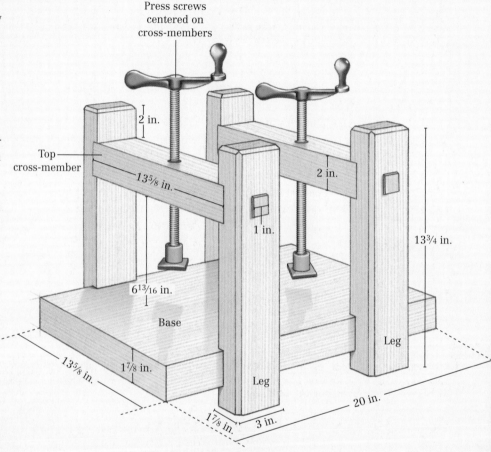

Press screws centered on cross-members

Top cross-member

2 in.

13⅝ in.

2 in.

1 in.

13¾ in.

6¹³⁄₁₆ in.

Base

Leg

13⅝ in.

1⅞ in.

Leg

1⅞ in.

3 in.

20 in.

C U T · L I S T			
LEGS	4	1⅞ IN. × 3 IN. × 13¾ IN.
CROSS-MEMBERS	2	2 IN. × 3 IN. × 16⅛ IN.
BASE	1	1⅞ IN. × 13⅝ IN. × 20 IN.
PRESS SCREWS	2	9 IN.

1. Saw the edges of the lap joint in the base and legs. Label the leg and corresponding joint in case of slight discrepancies in the parts. 2. Use a chisel to remove the waste between the sawcuts and then refine the depth with a router plane. 3. Dry-fit and check for square.

CUTTING THE HOUSED THROUGH TENONS

Mark the housed area in the tops of the legs where the cross-members will rest. This part of the joint is executed the same as the lap, with sawcuts made to establish the width of the cavity and the waste removed with chisel and router plane. Once the housed area is established for all four legs, mark the through tenon on both the inside and outside of each leg. With a brace and bit, begin from one side of each leg and bore down about halfway. Turn the piece over and bore in to complete

the holes. Square off the mortises using a chisel.

To mark the through tenons, insert the end of each cross-member into the housed area of the joint, and working from the outside of the through mortise, carefully mark the tenon locations.

I follow with a marking gauge to refine the pencil lines, making sure they're accurate and square to the cross-members. Saw out the tenons and test-fit the joints.

Depending on the size of the press screws you use, check the required diameter of the holes needed and bore

them out, centered on each cross-member. Install the screws as per the manufacturer's recommendations.

You can easily alter this design by adding as many or as few screws as you see fit for your specific application. With the joinery complete and the screws installed, go ahead and dry-fit the components. Chamfer the legs and glue the press together. Screws or wooden dowels can be added through the joinery for added strength.

4. Mark the mortises for the through tenons on both sides of the legs. 5. Drill through from both sides until the holes meet in the middle and then square up the mortises with some chisel work. 6. Insert the cross-member through the leg and mark the tenon from the outside. 7. Sawn and ready for clean-up. 8. A good fit for a rock-solid joint.

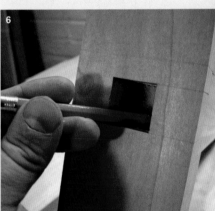

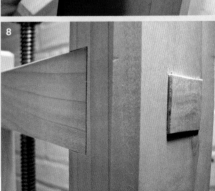

THE CARD CATALOG

"Made by hand, the craft object bears the fingerprints, real or metaphorical, of the person who fashioned it. These fingerprints are a sign, an almost invisible scar."

—Octavio Paz

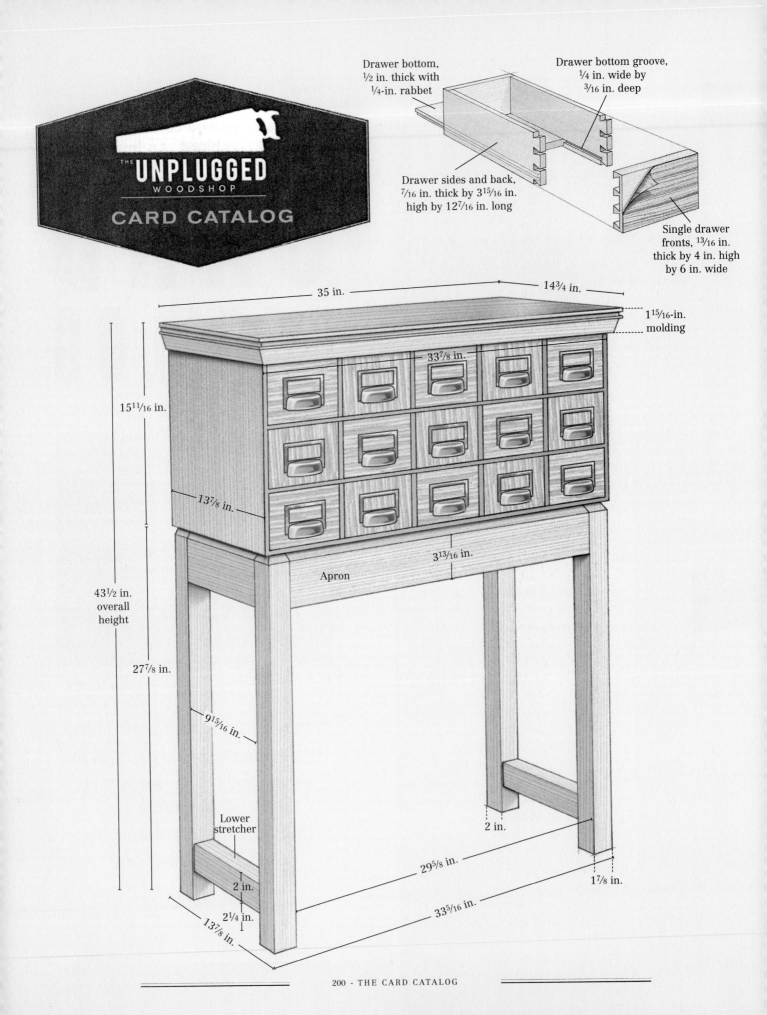

Drawer bottom, ½ in. thick with ¼-in. rabbet

Drawer bottom groove, ¼ in. wide by 3/16 in. deep

Drawer sides and back, 7/16 in. thick by 3 15/16 in. high by 12 7/16 in. long

Single drawer fronts, 13/16 in. thick by 4 in. high by 6 in. wide

THE UNPLUGGED WOODSHOP

CARD CATALOG

35 in.

14¾ in.

1 15/16-in. molding

33 7/8 in.

15 11/16 in.

13 7/8 in.

3 13/16 in.

Apron

43½ in. overall height

27 7/8 in.

9 15/16 in.

Lower stretcher

2 in.

2 in.

2¼ in.

13 7/8 in.

29 5/8 in.

1 7/8 in.

33 5/16 in.

At first glance, it looks as though the catalog were configured with three rows of five drawers each. Opening it up tells a different story, with five across the top, three in the middle, and one wide drawer at the bottom.

FOR THE FIRST 20 years of my life, my mother worked as a librarian. I realized at an early age how fortunate I was and spent many happy hours exploring the mysteries of the stacks. Aside from the books, of course, I was also fascinated by the humble card catalog. At the time, it seemed like one of the most enduring symbols of the library, but now, with the advance of all things digital, it has gone the way of the dodo . . . well almost.

Coincidentally, 12 years ago my wife came home from work and said the public school she was teaching at was throwing out some of the old catalog cabinets. We jumped in our then daily driver, a 1972 VW Kombi, and chugged up to the Dumpster® behind the school. We managed to salvage two of the cabinets and have been using one in our kitchen in Cape Breton ever since. It's been a wonderful piece to keep the kitchen tidy and stylin' at the same time, a great home for cutlery, kitchen utensils,

and all of those strange kitchen gadgets you find yourself gathering and collecting.

At 43½ in. high, this new cabinet design lends itself well to a variety of kitchen work where the extra height is beneficial for specific tasks. Bear this in mind when you're designing the molding profile. Maybe a butcher-block top would work, especially for a kitchen application. For a home office or study, this design would make an attractive sideboard. The list goes on and on, from funky wine storage for the vintage/modern pantry, to a fine lingerie cabinet in a walk-in closet or master suite reading nook area. There are a lot of great ideas for this piece and I'm sure you'll find a few more.

The design of this card catalog is based on the memories I carry from those early days exploring these wonderful cabinets in my mother's library. I knew straight away going into this piece that having 15 drawers wasn't practical for my storage needs, so I designed

CARCASE

Top and bottom panels .... 2 ...... 3/4 in. × 13 15/16 in. × 33 7/16 in.

Side panels .... 2 ...... 3/4 in. × 13 15/16 in. × 15 3/4 in.

Front molding .... 1 ...... 7/8 in. × 2 in. × 35 in.

Side molding .... 2 ...... 7/8 in. × 2 in. × 14 3/4 in.

INTERIOR CABINET

Drawer stretchers (front) .... 3 ...... 1/2 in. × 2 in. × 32 13/16 in.

Drawer runners .... 10 ...... 1/2 in. × 2 in. × 11 1/2 in.

Drawer stretchers (back) ..... 2 ...... 1/2 in. × 1 1/2 in. × 32 1/8 in.

Drawer dividers .... 6 ...... 1/2 in. × 2 in. × 4 1/4 in.

Drawer guides .... 6 ...... 7/16 in. × 3 7/8 in. × 10 in.

Filler strip .... 1 ...... 3/4 in. × 3/4 in. × 32 in. (sized to fit opening)

BACK PANEL

Top and bottom rails .... 2 ...... 3/4 in. × 2 7/8 in. × 30 1/4 in.

End stiles .... 2 ...... 3/4 in. × 2 7/8 in. × 14 5/8 in.

Center stile .... 1 ...... 3/4 in. × 2 7/8 in. × 11 3/4 in.

Panels .... 2 ...... 3/16 in. × 9 1/8 in. × 12 in.

STAND

Legs .... 4 ...... 1 7/8 in. × 2 in. × 27 7/8 in.

Front and back aprons .... 2 ...... 7/8 in. × 3 7/8 in. × 32 in.

Side aprons .... 2 ...... 7/8 in. × 3 7/8 in. × 12 5/8 in.

Lower stretchers .... 2 ...... 1 1/2 in. × 2 in. × 12 5/8 in.

Upper cross-stretchers .... 2 ...... 3/4 in. × 1 3/4 in. × 12 7/8 in.

SINGLE DRAWERS

Fronts .... 6 ...... 3/4 in. × 6 in. × 4 in.

Backs .... 6 ...... 7/16 in. × 6 in. × 4 in.

Sides .... 12 ...... 7/16 in. × 4 in. × 12 7/16 in.

Bottoms .... 6 ...... 1/2 in. × 5 5/16 in. × 11 7/8 in.

DOUBLE DRAWERS

Fronts .... 2 ...... 3/4 in. × 4 in. × 12 1/2 in.

Backs .... 2 ...... 7/16 in. × 4 in. × 12 1/2 in.

Sides .... 4 ...... 7/16 in. × 4 in. × 12 7/16 in.

Bottoms .... 2 ...... 1/2 in. × 11 7/8 in. × 11 7/8 in.

FIVE-DRAWER BANK

Front .... 1 ...... 3/4 in. × 4 in. × 32 in.

Back .... 1 ...... 7/16 in. × 4 in. × 32 in.

Sides .... 2 ...... 7/16 in. × 4 in. × 12 7/16 in.

Bottom .... 1 ...... 1/2 in. × 11 7/8 in. × 31 3/16 in.

Drawer front veneer .... 1/32 in. × 3 sq. ft. (approx.)

False drawer dividers .... 6 ...... 1/16 in. × 1/2 in. × 4 in.

Drawer stops .... 6 ...... 1/8 in. × 3/4 in. × 3 in.

Drawer stops .... 4 ...... 1/8 in. × 3/4 in. × 6 in.

Card frame pulls .... 15 ...... available from Lee Valley Tools (item # 01A5765)

JUST AROUND 1860, a Harvard librarian came up with a design that gave the public a means of accessing a card catalog. It used wooden blocks like book ends to keep the cards in order.

In 1877, the Cooperation Committee of the American Library Association Report made recommendations for standardized catalog cards. A handful of variations appeared but most libraries adopted the recommended new standard system.

By 1925, the card catalog cabinet had evolved into a uniform system, widely used throughout North America. The catalog cabinet served its purpose well and stood proud in libraries for generations until it was eventually replaced by the Online Public Access Catalog (OPAC).

Today, you'll find catalog cabinets at antiques venders and vintage furniture stores and although their original utilitarian use has run its course, these stately pieces are wonderful for many modern-day storage solutions.

MAKING THE CARCASE

The first step is to dimension the rough stock and make up the panels for the carcase. If you have wide boards, use them. If not, make up the panels from whatever widths you have on hand (see the photo below). The top and bottom carcase panels should finish at $33\frac{7}{16}$ in. long by $13\frac{15}{16}$ in. wide by $\frac{3}{4}$ in. thick, while the two side panels are $15\frac{3}{4}$ in. long by $13\frac{15}{16}$ in. wide by $\frac{3}{4}$ in. thick. Glue the assembly and plane the jointed panels flush. Once the glue cures, lay out the dovetails.

CUTTING THE CARCASE DOVETAILS
There are a lot of dovetails to cut for this cabinet so I'm going to make them all relatively wide. If you prefer, spend some time on the dovetails and make them as thin as you'd like. Either way is fine and structurally sound.

To begin, set a pair of dividers for the width of the outside half-pins. Register the divider off each end of the workpiece and leave a small reference mark at each end (see photo 1 on p. 204).

Next, take an estimated guess at how many dovetails you'll want in the piece, and set a second pair of dividers to the width of one tail plus a pin. (A safe guess is about a tail per inch.) Using the second pair of dividers, start from one of the end points you just made and lightly walk the dividers across the edge of the workpiece until you reach the opposite edge, being careful not to leave any marks just yet.

this version with only 9 drawers. It has 5 card-size drawers across the top, with a 6th card-size drawer in the center of the middle bank. The middle drawer is flanked by 2 double-size drawers, and the bottom 5-drawer bank is actually 1 large drawer. You can make all 15 or make only 3 if that would suit your needs better.

A seed bank might be a perfect use for this design. In fact, you could add three more banks of drawers above this set and use the piece as a card catalog! But really, who needs them anymore? Ironically enough, card pulls are still available through many online distributors, even though card catalog cabinets aren't being manufactured anymore. We're about to change that.

I used a medley of mismatched planks from previous projects for the carcase and was able to make the cabinet top with only one center joint. You may have to make the panels from narrower planks; that's fine, just a little bit more handwork to do.

When you reach the opposite side, take note of where the dividers land in relation to the reference mark on the opposite edge. Your dividers should overstep this point and finish off a little past it (¼ in. at most). This small space will represent the width of the pins when you mark them. If this pin width looks good to you, go ahead and walk back across the end grain leaving marks as you go.

When you reach the opposite end, lay the dividers in the other reference mark and step back across the workpiece, leaving marks. These marks, every inch or so across the end grain, represent the width of your pins and are used to register your pencil when laying out the tails. Lay out and cut the dovetails as shown in the photos on the facing page.

The bottom dovetails are laid out exactly the same as the top and at the same time. In fact, the reason we use two sets of dividers is for continuity between these parts. Set one divider for the end pins, and the other for the tails.

ROUTING THE INTERIOR DADOES

Once you have the dovetails cleaned up, do a dry-fit to see how they go together. Don't mash them all the way together just yet—this is just a quick test to see if they'll do for now. You'll fine-tune the dovetails when you get the four corners of the carcase complete.

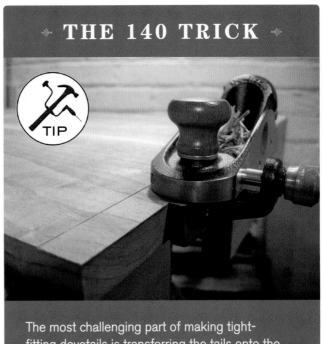

THE 140 TRICK

TIP

The most challenging part of making tight-fitting dovetails is transferring the tails onto the pin board, and the traditional way to make that process a little easier is to use the "140 trick." This handy trick gets its name from the Stanley® No. 140 rabbet plane and simply involves cutting a shallow rabbet (¹⁄₃₂ in. deep at the very most) on the inside of the tail boards before you start cutting your dovetails. This creates a small shelf at the base of the tails that makes transferring the tails onto the pin board a little easier.

1. Beginning at the outside corners, mark the half-pins on each end. 2. After stepping across the edge, your dividers should finish a little beyond the half-pin mark you made earlier. This distance will represent the width of each pin when you lay them out.

1. Using a dovetail marker or bevel gauge, pencil in the dovetails working off of the marks you just made. 2. After marking the tails, saw down each of the lines, making sure not to cut past the bottom shoulder line. 3. Remove the waste from between the tails with a fretsaw, leaving as little material as you can. Chop out the remaining waste with a chisel. 4. Rotate the board to the horizontal position and saw the two outside shoulders of the tail board. 5. Scribe the tails onto the ends of the pin boards. This is where the 140 trick pays off. 6. Scribble in the waste area and rip down the sides of the pins. 7. Remove the waste with a fretsaw and then finish with a chisel.

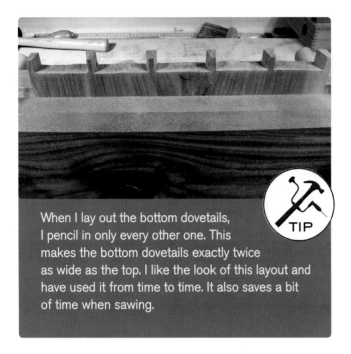

When I lay out the bottom dovetails, I pencil in only every other one. This makes the bottom dovetails exactly twice as wide as the top. I like the look of this layout and have used it from time to time. It also saves a bit of time when sawing.

Now disassemble the dry-fit panels and lay out the dadoes for the interior drawer frames (the drawer stretchers and four of the drawer runners will mate with these). Scribe the sides of the interior dadoes and use a chisel to create a small V-groove so the router plane can begin removing the waste. (You could also set up a makeshift fence and saw down the sides of the dado with a backsaw to establish the sides.) Take a series of passes and plow the dadoes to a consistent depth (see the photo below).

MAKING THE DRAWER STRETCHERS, RUNNERS, AND DIVIDERS

With the dadoes complete on the inside of the carcase panels, dimension the stock for the interior components (including the false drawer dividers that you'll need later in the build; see p. 223). The face-frame components are made from 2-in. walnut, while the interior parts are a secondary wood; in this case, poplar. Dimension the stock to ½-in. thickness. The widths of the runners and stretchers are slightly differ-

A router plane makes it easy to plow the carcase dadoes to a consistent depth. Use a chisel to create a small V-groove to guide the router plane.

1. Shape the sliding dovetails on the front stretchers with a series of sawcuts. They'll slide into a 1½-in.-deep socket cut into the inside cabinet sides. 2. Scribe the dovetail sockets directly off the stretchers. I used an offcut dimensioned to my drawer height to set the distance between the stretchers.

ent, so refer to the cut list after thicknessing your stock and rip the interior parts to width.

FITTING THE STRETCHERS

Next, crosscut the interior parts and rough-dimension the front walnut drawer stretchers and dividers. The front drawer stretchers join to the carcase sides with sliding dovetails, which add a great deal of rigidity to the cabinet. Lay these out and cut them next. Start with the sloping, ripsaw cuts to establish the sides of the dovetail. Then make the shoulder cuts to remove the waste. Clean up the back of the stretcher where the dovetail meets the stub tenon. This stub tenon will mate with the dado we just finished in the previous step. The width of the front drawer stretchers is 1¹⁵⁄₁₆-in. I made the dovetailed portion 1½ in. deep with the remaining width at the back making up the stub tenon (see photo 1 above).

Slip the stretchers into the corresponding dadoes on the inside of the cabinet sides. The stub tenons will get you started and then the back of the dovetail will hit the front edge of

the cabinet and stop the stretcher from going in any farther. Hold the stretcher in this position, making sure it's square to the sides, and scribe the dovetails onto the front edge of the cabinet. Remove the waste as you would any half-blind dovetail. Make the two outside sawcuts and chisel away the waste. I used a router plane to get a consistent depth along the socket bottom.

Dry-fit the stretchers. At this point, leave them a little proud; you'll plane them flush after assembly.

CUTTING THE RUNNERS

Now mark and cut the joinery for the rear stretchers and the drawer runners. This entails a lot of small-scale mortise-and-tenon work so get comfortable, sharpen your chisels, and get at it. The rear drawer stretchers receive stub tenons into the cabinet side dadoes, and the drawer runners are all mortised and tenoned where they meet the front and back stretchers.

After the tenons are sawn in all of the runners, lay out the long side tenons on the four outside runners. These long tenons will join the interior dadoes on the carcase interior. Now mark the mating mortises on the stretchers. To make the layout a little faster, I took a few minutes to make a story stick (see p. 209).

Also mark the back stretchers. Once again, continuity between the front and back stretchers is important. The runners will all sit square to the frame and carcase if you work carefully and cleanly.

Whenever possible, lay out multiple pieces together (here, the tenons on the drawer runners). This not only saves time but also helps for continuity sake in the runners. You'll notice the first runner at the far right of the group already has tenons. This was my test piece that the rest of the group will be laid out from. I made sure the runner worked in all positions inside the carcase beforehand.

1. The four outside runners need a long tenon, or tongue, down their outside edges, to mate with the interior carcase dadoes. Remove the bulk of the material with a rabbet plane and fine-tune with a shoulder plane. 2. The drawer runners complete: six interior and four for the sides. Now they're ready to go and meet some mortises! 3. Transfer the story stick's story onto the stretchers (say that five times fast!). 4. Boring a series of ¼-in. holes makes quick work of the mortises. After some chiseling, the dry-fit begins.

1. Dry-assemble the two frames and press them in place inside the cabinet. At this point it has no drawer dividers or guides; those are next. 2. The bottom stub tenon on each drawer divider meets the stopped dado in the stretcher. 3. Dry-fit the stretchers and the six dividers and you'll see the drawer configuration take shape. I decided not to make all 15 drawers; instead this cabinet has 9 drawers. When you make the drawers you'll attach false dividers on the drawer fronts to keep the traditional card catalog appearance.

Bore out the waste on each of the mortises and square them up with some chisel work. Label each part as you go and remember, these don't have to be super pretty; they're inside the cabinet where no one will see them. Now dry-assemble the two frames and press them in place inside the cabinet.

FITTING THE DIVIDERS

Using the story stick, transfer the locations for the stopped dadoes where the drawer dividers meet the stretchers. These are only $1/16$ in. deep and will be made over the mortises you just finished. Deep scribe lines, a router plane, and a chisel are all you need to make these shallow stopped dadoes in the stretchers. Take your time executing these dadoes so you don't blow out the thin material between the two.

CUTTING THE RABBET FOR THE CABINET BACK

It seems that many hand-tool users shy away from cutting stopped rabbet joints. I'm not sure why because I think they're easy to execute with only a crosscut saw and some chisel work. Begin by scribing the rabbet on the inside back of the panels. The rabbet should be $1/8$ in. wide and $1/2$ in. deep and stop at the baselines of the

✦ A STORY STICK ✦

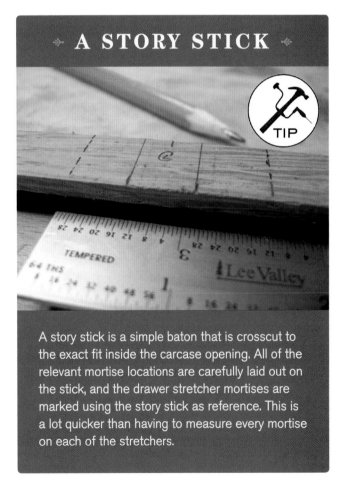

A story stick is a simple baton that is crosscut to the exact fit inside the carcase opening. All of the relevant mortise locations are carefully laid out on the stick, and the drawer stretcher mortises are marked using the story stick as reference. This is a lot quicker than having to measure every mortise on each of the stretchers.

side dovetails. Using a crosscut saw, make a series of relief cuts along the rabbet and then simply clean away the waste with a chisel. Square up the corners and test-fit the parts.

The inside edges of the frame and panel back will also be rabbeted (see the next section). This will make a stronger carcase once the back panel is in place. These surfaces will also be cleaned up and fine-tuned.

MAKING THE BACK PANEL

The back panel is straightforward, frame-and-panel construction. Mortise-and-tenon joinery holds the frame together, while a $3/16$-in. panel floats inside grooves planed into the panel stiles and rails. The tenons in the top and bottom rails as well as the middle stile are $1\frac{7}{8}$ in. long by $2\frac{1}{8}$ in. wide by $\frac{1}{4}$ in. thick. Lay these out next.

Cut a $\frac{1}{4}$-in. groove, about $\frac{3}{16}$ in. deep for the panel in the frame parts (see photo 2 on the facing page). I offset the groove from center

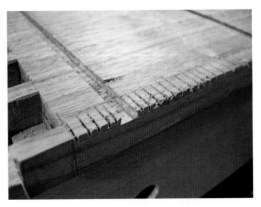

Begin the rabbet for the back panel by making a series of sawcuts along the area to be rabbeted, trying not to saw past the scribe lines. Note that the rabbet begins and ends at the baseline for the dovetails.

because I didn't want a wide ledge across the bottom of the panel, which would only catch dust. The offset groove for the cabinet back will keep this ledge to a minimum, and a bead scratched in a few of the inside edges will finish the deal.

I scratched a bead around the inside middle of the frame. Although this is the back of the

Clean up the waste with a large chisel, define the shoulders with some lighter chisel work, and then dry-fit the carcase.

1. The back panel is straightforward, frame-and-panel construction. A quick coat of shellac at this point protects the part during the build. 2. Plow a 3/16-in.-deep groove for the back panel in the frame parts. 3. A dry-fit after shellac; note the bead scratched around the inside middle of the frame. 4. Dry-fit the drawer guides inside the carcase; they will be glued to the front dividers and lower runners only. The tops are allowed to "float" to accommodate wood movement.

cabinet and no one may ever see it, I think it's good practice to build your furniture as if it were destined for the very center of the room. Someday in the future, someone may be looking at the back of this cabinet and when they do, they'll see that the artisan who crafted this piece cared enough to consider how the back of the cabinet looked.

Scribe the rabbet onto the inside of the frame where it meets the inside rabbet on the cabinet back. The back panel rabbet should finish at 1/4 in. wide by 7/16 in. deep. After test-fitting the panel, I gave it a quick coat of shellac to protect the pieces while I continue along in the build.

MAKING THE DRAWER GUIDES

After the back panel is complete, make up the stock for the six drawer guides, which should finish at 10 in. long by 3 7/8 in. wide by 7/16 in. thick. The drawer guides will be glued only along the bottom and front to allow for wood movement. The drawer guide stock is finished a hair thinner than the front walnut dividers. If you make this cabinet in the winter and

1. Plane the dovetails flush after the glue sets, using a steel straightedge to check for flat as you work. You'd be surprised at how little it takes to make this edge concave or convex. 2. Glue the drawer dividers and front stretchers on the benchtop. Note that because there are three drawer banks, the middle dividers won't be able to receive screws because the top dividers are in the way. These will get toenailed after assembly using small finish nails. 3. Glue the drawer face frame into the sliding dovetails in the carcase panels.

expect the drawer guides to swell a little when it warms up, leave some room and dimension them accordingly. They don't have to go all the way to the top of the drawer slots.

GLUING THE CARCASE

After the interior components are complete and dry-fit, disassemble the pieces and get ready for the glue-up. I used liquid hide glue for the main carcase as it has a longer open time. Apply glue to both sides of the dovetails and knock the panels together. Take some diagonal inside corner measurements after you get the panels together to make sure they are sitting square. Once the glue sets up, plane the dovetails flush and clean up the carcase. Any difficult grain can be dressed with a smoothing plane and/or card scraper.

GLUING AND SCREWING THE DRAWER STRETCHERS AND DIVIDERS

When the carcase is cleaned up, glue the drawer dividers and stretchers together on the benchtop. They will be assembled and then inserted into the carcase as one complete unit. I used hot hide glue for this application; the shorter open time is beneficial when working with this many parts. I apply glue to the divider, hold it in place for a few moments, and then move on to the next. Each stretcher receives the dividers in sequence and screws are added to reinforce the joint. Predrill the screw holes beforehand!

Once the stretchers and dividers are one complete unit, glue the entire assembly into the main carcase. I laid the cabinet on its back to allow gravity to work with me. A rubber mallet and a few light taps pressed the face frame into place. The top of the cabinet has a ¾-in. gap between the top stretcher and the cabinet top. I cut a strip to fill in this space; it is also glued and screwed to the carcase top at this stage. This filler strip, along with the top stretcher and cabinet top edge, will be covered by the molding later on.

Glue the drawer runners in place next. I work from left to right and apply hot hide glue to one end at a time. After all the runners are pressed into the front stretcher, I apply glue to the rear tenons and install the rear stretcher. Again working from left to right, I push the first tenon in a little and work my way across, holding the stretcher in place while I line up the row of runners. This is a bit of a balancing act, but once the tenons are in a little, I start applying some clamping pressure and draw the rear stretcher in as one. Try to keep it level as you go and make sure you don't push the front stretcher out of the sliding dovetails. Check as you go.

Remove a little at a time when using a router plane. I became impatient when cutting the dadoes on the inside of the cabinet and started taking too heavy a cut and got some bad tearout. Luckily, the drawers and interior frame will cover it all. Light passes are safer with hand tools. Both for you and your work.

TIP

Gluing the lower assembly of runners and rear stretchers inside the carcase.

1. Cut a paper template and mark the molding profile. 2. For the initial molding, a plow plane begins the excavation and establishes the first groove, or fillet, at the top of the molding profile. Follow with a rabbet or moving fillister plane to knock down the main face of the molding. From here, three more rabbets were made to define the bead along the bottom. 3. After the rabbets are made, molding planes are used for the inside round areas. 4. Dry-fit the sides of the molding and fine-tune the front for a perfect fit.

Because each of the drawer dividers sits on top of the other dividers, I wasn't able to install screws in the middle dividers earlier. I toenailed them in place with some small finish nails (after predrilling the holes with a gimlet).

MAKING THE MOLDING

When I originally sketched this design, I drew moldings along the carcase top and bottom. I decided to add only the top molding and ended up making four different samples before going with the final profile you see in the finished piece.

Molding is like icing on a cake and you can decide what flavor best suits your decor. I started making a 2-in.-thick, traditional-style molding and decided it was too heavy looking for the piece. I then ripped the stock down to 1 in. and made a second profile. After that, I decided to update it as well, for a slightly more contemporary feel.

Rough-saw the stock for the molding. Use the straightest grain you can and take it from a plank long enough to wrap around the cabinet sides and front. Grain wrapping around carefully mitered corners is a nice touch. Dress the molding stock until it's "square six sides" (S6S).

After you design and draw the molding profile at both ends of the stock, scribe whatever series of rabbets and/or grooves works best to remove the waste in the profile (90% of the waste material is removed with plow, rabbet, moving fillister, and/or shoulder plane). Think about each step and each groove. Consider the plane you'll use and how it needs to ride against something. Maybe you'll need to plow a groove and then the rabbet? Once the rough work is done, use the molding planes to refine the shape and add the rounds or hollows.

A few more molding planes were used to remove the waste area. The different widths of the hollow molding planes, helped define the *gentler* area of the hollow. This inside curve is more oval in shape. A curved scraper and finally some sanding blended the curve, removed the plane tracks, and finished the profile.

Miter the molding on a shopmade miter box. Rough-cut a length for the side, then the front, and then the other side for grain continuity around the corners. Leave them a little heavy and clean them up with a handplane, shooting board, and/or a miter jack.

I like the look of the molding shown in the photos on the facing page, especially for a piece that has a vintage look, but after a few hours of work, I decided I wanted a more contemporary molding and ended up making another one. The new molding is a little less traditional but the process of manufacturing it was the same. Lay out the profile and then the series of grooves and rabbets needed to rough out the basic shape. Use the hollows and rounds, or any dedicated profile you may have, and fine-tune the shape.

MAKING THE STAND

The legs of the stand are made from 2-in. roughsawn walnut. Pay close attention to the patterns hiding in the wood grain and try to

Whenever you make custom molding, try to design the profiles using the molding planes you already have in your kit. If you have only one hollow and one round, then a simple curved shape with top fillet or rabbet may work. The point is, use what you have and be as creative as you can be.

lay out the furniture parts with those patterns in mind. If possible, lay out the leg stock from an area of the plank where the end grain runs diagonally across its width. The result will be a leg that has a more uniform grain pattern on all four sides instead of rift-sawn on two and flatsawn on the opposite two.

The aprons are taken from the same stock as the legs. The plank is 2 in. thick, which means I have to resaw it. I treat this cut like any ripcut. Mark the line, take a deep breath, and start sawing. Rotate the plank every few inches to maintain a straight cut. (Note that at this point, I hadn't completed my frame saw, [see p. 130];

The legs are made from 2-in. roughsawn walnut.

8/4 walnut for the aprons.

it would have been a whole lot easier to use the kerfing plane and frame saw combo to do this step. Trust me: resawing with a panel saw is possible, but not much fun for anything over a few inches wide. The length is almost irrelevant, it's the width that gets you.) Crosscut the plank for the aprons long so you'll get one short side and one long from each side. The

grain will match up well around the corners of the stand.

To begin the stand joinery, clean and square the ends of the legs. Once they are cut to length, mark out the necessary mortise-and-tenon joinery. The apron tenons are 1½ in. long by 2½ in. wide by ½ in. thick. If they were any wider, I'd break them into two tenons, but for this application one 2½-in. tenon will suffice. The mortises will be offset so the

1. Saw the tenons in the apron stock. I use a 14-in. ripsaw for this size joinery. 2. Offset the mortises for the apron tenons in the legs.

WORKING AHEAD

WHILE IN ROUGH-STOCK mode, I also made up the drawer sides and backs. For these I used some curly maple I'd had in my shop for a few years. It had been resawn to ½ in. and was stable. Make up your drawer stock as early in the project as possible. This will give you a few days or even weeks to let it sit. About 90% of the stock I use for these projects is seasoned in my shop for a minimum of nine months. In every case, the stock was purchased already dry.

aprons will finish flush with the outside of the legs. (If you'd prefer a small recess, then step the aprons back a little and adjust the joinery to suit.) The inside of the tenons will meet inside the legs so you'll have to miter the ends slightly. Refer to "Stand Joinery" below for details.

After marking the mortises, remove the waste with a brace and bit and square things up with some chisel work. Dry-fit the parts as you go and label the mating mortise and tenons. You'll need to cut a miter on the tenon ends. You could simply cut one tenon shorter but I decided to miter each one to keep the maximum length on each. The tenon could also be notched where it meets the other. I've seen a few alternate ways of executing the ends of tenons when they meet inside a leg or post. One was a kind of half-lap joint and another was a

through tenon affair. Do some research and see what you find. This method works fine for this scale of work.

⊰ 22 REVOLUTIONS? ⊱

That's how many revolutions, or turns, it takes me to reach my depth while boring out the 1½-in.-deep mortises in the legs. Instead of marking the bit with painter's tape or using some elaborate mechanical device, I count the revolutions needed to reach my mortise depth. It took me 22 full turns on the brace, so for the rest of the holes, I'm able to count revolutions and not worry about the depth.

TIP

STAND JOINERY

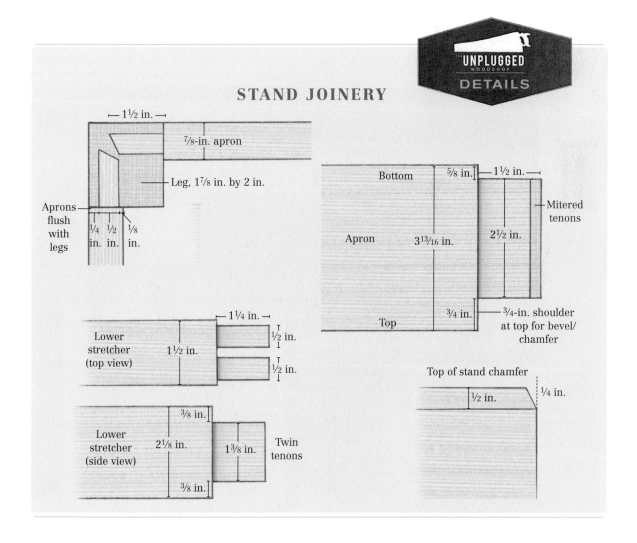

UNPLUGGED WOODSHOP
DETAILS

Both apron tenon ends need to be mitered to fit where they meet inside the leg mortise.

After the top apron joinery is complete and dry-fit, lay out and cut the lower tenon joinery for the bottom stretchers. I decided to use twin tenons for this application because the twin tenons will add strength and keep the stand from any wracking.

With the tenons complete in the lower stretchers, mark the matching mortises in the bottom of the legs. As always, a brace and bit removes the waste with some quick chisel work to square them up. Dry-fit the stand once complete, and if everything looks good, clean up the parts and glue the two end assemblies.

Before gluing the front and back aprons to join the side assemblies, chamfer the top edges of the stand. This is easier to do now before the full stand is assembled. The side gables are also chamfered. This chamfer

The lower stretchers on the stand are joined to the legs with twin tenons (1¼ in. long and ½ in. wide).

Glue up the two ends first and then add the front and back aprons. Working this way makes the glue-up a little less stressful.

After the top cross-stretcher lap joints are complete and you've dry-fit the parts, glue the front and back aprons. Glue the cross-stretchers in place next. The cross-stretchers will be screwed to the stand and elongated holes will be drilled in them to attach the carcase. I made two slots in each cross-member about 3 in. in from each apron. The carcase wood grain runs end to end, so these screw holes need to be elongated to allow the carcase to move seasonally.

MAKING THE DRAWERS

Once the stand is complete, it's time to move onto the drawer fronts in the cabinet. As mentioned earlier, I'm making only 9 drawers in this cabinet but once complete, it'll look as if there were 15. Traditional half-blind dovetails in the drawer fronts and through dovetails at the back will keep these drawers together for generations of use. The drawer bottoms are made from solid ½-in stock. Each drawer bottom is raised with a tongue to slide into a ¼-in. groove on the drawer interior.

I used a mish-mash of walnut offcuts from past projects for the drawer faces. They'll all be

creates a visual relief between the top of the stand and the cabinet carcase. It isn't structural but only an aesthetic touch. I like the shadow lines it creates and adds another element to the design.

ADDING THE CROSS-STRETCHERS

Two interior cross-stretchers, joined to the front and back aprons with simple lap joints, give something solid to attach the cabinet carcase to the stand. Crosscut the cross-stretchers and lay out the joinery.

1. Place the cross-stretcher on the inside of the stand and scribe the lap on the top of the apron. 2. The interior cross-stretchers reinforce the stand and give something solid to attach the carcase to.

1. The nine drawer fronts sized to the openings. Make the fronts a tight fit at this point; they'll be fine-tuned later in the build. 2. Use two pine templates to mark and fit the drawer sides. 3. The drawer components are ready for dovetails after all of the parts have been carefully fit to the drawer openings.

veneered, so it's only the end grain for the half-blind dovetails I'm concerned with aesthetically. If you don't plan on veneering the drawer fronts, make them from matching grain and sequence them from the same plank as you go.

The drawer-making process goes like this: Fit the drawer fronts and scribe the backs off of them. (If you're not veneering the drawer fronts, fit the backs first and scribe the fronts off of them. That way, if you mess up a part, you won't lose the continuity in the drawer-front grain pattern but will only have to remake the back.) Once the fronts and backs are fit, move to the sides. I work across a drawer bank, keeping the parts together as I go, marking with builder's triangles to keep all the drawer parts in line. To eliminate a bit of measuring, I made up two pine templates for the drawer sides that I use to quickly scribe the maple stock when making up the rest of the sides (see photo 2 above).

As you lay out the stock for your drawer parts, watch for grain direction and mark the pieces as you work through every step. Make sure the grain direction of the drawer sides runs front to back. This will prevent you from damaging the dovetails after glue-up when you're fitting the drawers.

CUTTING HALF-BLIND DOVETAILS

The first step when cutting the half-blind dovetails is to cut the grooves for the drawer bottom using a plow plane (see photo 1 on the facing page). These ¼-in. grooves are cut about ¼ in. up from the drawer bottoms. The drawer backs will be ripped to width and the drawer bottom panel will slide into this groove from underneath.

After the drawer bottom grooves are complete, use your dividers and lay out the dovetails on the drawer sides. Because I have so many of these to do, I made them fairly wide, with just three dovetails per side. You could make them smaller with only a sawkerf between them: These are only aesthetic decisions and won't affect the structural integrity of the drawer. Rip-cut the slopes of the tails and then remove the waste with a fretsaw. Transfer the tails to the pin board and chop away the waste in the sockets.

After chopping all of the half-blind dovetails in the drawer fronts, the back through dovetails will feel like a walk in the park. When you have the drawer components complete, you can start assembling. If you plan on adding face veneer, that's the next step. If you decide not to add veneer to the drawer fronts, you can move onto the drawer assembly after you've fine-tuned the parts and made up the drawer bottom stock.

VENEERING THE DRAWER FRONTS

To begin veneering, cut out the $1/32$-in.-thick veneer, leaving it about $1/8$ in. oversize to the drawer fronts (see the photo on p. 222). This zebrawood veneer is easy to work with a veneer saw, and in no time you'll have the 15 veneers cut and ready for hot hide glue. I

When transferring the tails to the pin board, make a small ¼-in. shim to slide into the drawer bottom groove. The shim will make it easy to line up the two parts. Use a wood block to hold up the drawer sides, and when you clamp your work, make sure it's set to the same height as the block you're using.

say 15 because the 9 drawers will still look like 15 when complete to keep the traditional look of the card catalog in check.

I decided to alternate the pattern on every other drawer to create something I hope is

1. Cut the ¼-in. drawer bottom grooves first, about ¼ in. up from the bottom of the sides and the drawer fronts.
2. Cut all the half-blind dovetails in the drawer fronts.

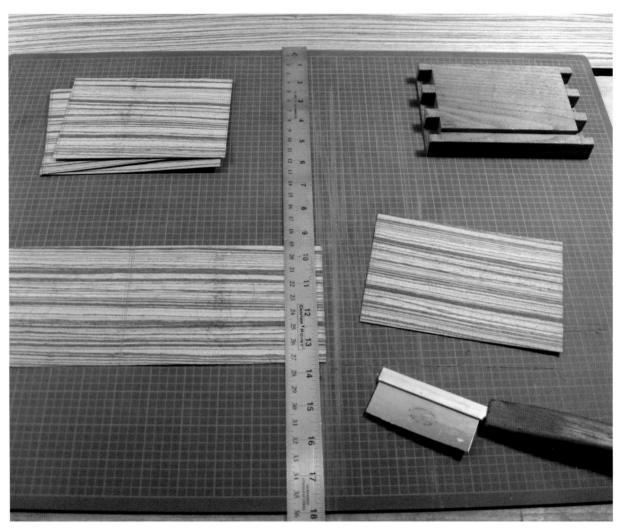

Size the zebrawood veneer for the drawer fronts.

quilt-like in feel (my crafty mom's influence again). I could spend many hours on the drawer fronts, perhaps using marquetry or parquetry, but that's for another day. Of course, a nice straight-grained hardwood would be better than fine. But I already had a group of mismatched walnut offcuts and thought it would be a responsible time to use as many of them as I could. The details dictate the design, and in this case, the drawer front veneer was my chosen option.

At this stage, rip some ⅛-in. strips off of each edge of the false drawer divider stock you roughed out earlier (see p. 206). This is easy and accurate to do with the kerfing plane.

Before applying the veneer to the drawer fronts, you need to tooth the surface. *Toothing*

It's well worth the extra few dollars to buy high-quality, thick veneer (in the ⅟₃₂-in. range). Discount veneer is widely available, but it's too thin for furniture making and there's a good chance of damaging it while working.

TIP

is the process of scratching small grooves into the surface that will make for a stronger glue bond. Toothing planes are no longer manufactured, but most handplane manufacturers offer some toothing irons for a few of their planes. Look around and you'll find them. I purchased an iron from Lee Valley Tools that fits their block plane perfectly.

APPLYING THE VENEER

Applying veneer using hot hide glue and a veneer hammer is pretty straightforward. Begin by masking the drawer sides with clear packing tape—the glue will be squeezed out from under the veneer and the drawer sides will get a little messy. Apply the veneer as explained and shown in "Veneering 101" photos on p. 224.

Fine-tuning the drawer-front edges is still possible once the veneer is applied. You just need to work carefully. Chisels, files, and sandpaper all work. I also used my shooting board as well as a dedicated sanding block.

FITTING THE FALSE DRAWER DIVIDERS

The false dividers that we ripped earlier need to be planed to their final thickness. Tolerances like this are easy with hand tools. A simple jig holds the piece in place, and when I reach somewhere in the 3/32-in. thickness, I'm done (see photo 1 on p. 225). Three or four passes are all it takes on the shooting board.

Tooth the *multiple-front* drawer fronts and glue each side of the face veneer separately to make the process easier. With the grain direction changing from one drawer front to the other, sanding and dressing after gluing will be easier without the divider in the way. Two C-clamps hold the divider in place while the face veneer is applied. Make sure you remove it as soon as the veneer is on or it'll be stuck as well!

Test-fit the drawer fronts and see how everything looks. If all is well, it's time to glue up the drawers. A good-fitting dovetailed drawer shouldn't need any clamping pressure after the glue is applied but if need be, throw on a clamp or two as you go. I used liquid hide glue on the drawers for the longer open time and worked my way across each drawer bank until the nine drawers were complete.

Once the glue sets, clean up any squeeze-out and plane the dovetails flush with the drawer sides. This shouldn't be a problem if you carefully laid out the drawer side stock earlier and made sure the wood grain on the drawer sides is running from front to back. If you missed that step, be careful when flush-

1. The false dividers are laid out in sequence to the "real" drawer dividers already in place. The grain flows through the parts thanks to the step you did earlier when roughing-out the stock from the same piece. Now after all that work, make sure to label everything and keep the parts in order. 2. Saw the false dividers with the kerfing plane. 3. Toothing the drawer fronts before veneering makes for a better glue bond.

VENEERING 101

THE KEY TO veneering is to work fast: don't engage in a conversation, and don't stop halfway through the process!

Make sure you clean up the toothing debris first. Small particles can get under the veneer and cause trouble. Spread a generous amount of hot glue over the drawer face. Next, lay the veneer face down in the glue and spread another layer of glue over the entire back of the veneer.

Carefully turn the veneer over and, using the veneer hammer like a squeegee, work all of the air, extra glue, and bubbles out from under the veneer. Pay close attention to the edges and try to work with the grain as much as possible.

After a minute or two of pushing, pulling, and pressing, you'll start to hear small crackling sounds as the glue begins to set. This is when you should stop. Lightly tap around the surface and then hold it up to the light to see if you have any bubbles, voids, cracks, dents, whatever—you know, trouble. If not, peel off the tape and set the drawer fronts aside to dry.

Clean off the edges before the glue is fully cured. I wait until after the next drawer is veneered and then jump back and clean the glue off of the first one. I'm always alternating between those two tasks until I have the drawer faces all veneered. Let the stack cure a little and then trim the veneer to final size.

1. Mask the sides of the drawer with clear tape to protect them from glue squeeze-out. 2. Apply the veneer using hot hide glue and a veneer hammer. 3. Trim the drawer fronts after the veneer has dried. 4. The pattern slowly emerges. The drawer pulls themselves will hide much of the grain, but alternating the grain pattern is a fun way to add some movement to the piece.

1. Thickness the false dividers using a simple jig on the shooting board. 2. With the top two veneered drawers dry-fit and pushed into finished depth, test-fit the middle double drawer to see if the thickness of the false drawer divider is accurate. If it looks good, get ready to veneer the double drawer and apply the false divider. 3. After toothing the double-wide drawers, dry-clamp the false divider in place and veneer each side of the drawer separately. 4. After the face veneer is applied to the drawer fronts, clean up the middle divider location before the false divider is glued in place. 5. With its four false dividers, five alternating wood grain veneers, and large width, the lower drawer front is the hardest to make. 6. With drawer front veneer complete and false dividers attached, it's hard to tell which drawers are real and which are false.

ing up the dovetails so you don't damage the face veneer or the half-lap on the drawer front edges.

After the drawer boxes are fit, "raise" the 1/2-in.-thick drawer bottoms so they fit the 1/4-in. drawer bottom grooves. I used a rabbet plane for this step and fine-tuned the fit with a shoulder plane.

After test-fitting the drawer fronts and seeing the cabinet on the stand, I decided a small chamfer on the bottom edge of the cabinet would make the transition between the carcase and stand a little more defined. Sometimes details are like that. You have to work them in along the way.

FINISHING THE CARD CATALOG

I used a super-blond shellac to finish the zebrawood veneer and dark garnet for the rest of the cabinet. Because the walnut I used for the carcase, stand, and drawer fronts all came from a few past projects, I hoped the dark shellac would bring the various shades a little closer together.

I buy my shellac in flakes and mix it myself with denatured alcohol. The process is easy and you can get the exact finish you want. This would be considered between a 1-lb. and 2-lb. cut.

Finish the drawer fronts with super-blond shellac and the false dividers with dark garnet.

Apply the shellac in continuous coats until the rubber (or pad) starts to drag. I let the shellac sit for a while and then give it a light rubbing with 320-grit sandpaper. Apply more shellac and continue the process until you're happy with the buildup of finish. When I have a lot of time to spend on finishing, I prefer to apply up to a dozen coats of a 1-lb. cut that's been thinned again so it's very light. This gives a more natural finish because the shellac seems to have the time and viscosity to work into the wood grain a little better. These light layers tend to keep the grain feeling more natural, while the 1½-lb. or 2-lb. cut is heavier and covers the grain to give more of a topcoat finish. Experiment between projects and fine-tune your finishes.

The drawer fronts with the false dividers are a bit trickier. The dividers need to have the dark garnet shellac applied before the veneered fronts get the blond shellac. Using an artist's brush, I carefully finished the dividers with the dark garnet before I coated the drawer fronts. If the blond gets on the dark, it's no problem. The other way around . . . not so much. Mask off the false dividers with card stock or painter's tape and apply the dark shellac.

ATTACHING THE HARDWARE
After finishing, apply the hardware. Make a template for the drawer pulls and use an awl to carefully mark the screw locations. Drill and countersink the drawer fronts for the two screws that come with the card pulls.

FITTING THE DRAWER STOPS
With the drawers all fit and finished and the hardware attached, you are just about done,

but adding drawer stops to each opening is a detail that can really make a difference. The drawer stops are applied on the lower inside front of each drawer opening so the drawer reveal will stay consistent through the seasons. If the carcase dimensions change with seasonal movement, the drawer fronts will always maintain the set reveal. Some woodworkers prefer to place the drawer stops at the back of the carcase but doing so means if the cabinet expands or contracts over time, the drawer reveal would change.

The drawer stops are made from thin 1/8-in. material about 3 in. long and 3/4 in. wide for the single drawers and about 6 in. long for the two double drawers. I used two more at 6 in. long for the full-width bottom drawer and

A hand drill is the perfect tool for drilling through veneer. You'll never feel if the veneer is hollowed or is chipping a little with a cordless drill. Try the egg beaters and see what I mean; you'll feel the wood grain while you're drilling.

placed them on the outside edges. These thin strips are glued in place just behind the depth of the drawer fronts after setting them to the desired reveal. When the drawers are closed, the bottom of the drawer fronts will hit these thin strips and stop the drawers exactly where you want them to.

The saw bench and a couple of surface clamps make a perfect work surface for working on the drawer front hardware.

1. Set the drawer for the desired reveal, make a mark on the stretcher, and then measure back the thickness of the drawer front. Glue the drawer stop at this point.
2. Rear screw slots in the carcase sides will allow the side panel to move while the molding will float.

ATTACHING THE MOLDING

To account for wood movement, I cut a slot for a screw at the back top corner of the cabinet side where the molding will attach. The molding is glued across the front of the cabinet, where wood movement isn't a problem because both parts run the same direction. But the cabinet sides will expand and contract and the moldings will not. The back of the side molding is held in place with a screw, which will be able to move along this slot as the cabinet sides change through the seasons.

Prefinish the moldings and apply, gluing the front molding and only the first few inches of the sides. The backs of the moldings are held in place by the sliding screws.

The mix of zebrawood drawer fronts and the silver hardware gives the piece a sense of timelessness. It could have sat in my mother's library 30 years ago or go just as well in our front hallway as an entry table tomorrow.

RESOURCES

These are the sources for the products I use in my shop.

LEE VALLEY TOOLS
Hand tools, hardware, and finishing supplies
www.leevalley.com

BAD AXE TOOL WORKS
Makers of the kerfing plane and frame-saw blades as well as fine handsaws
www.badaxetoolworks.com

TOOLS FOR WORKING WOOD
Bowsaw, hot glue pot, hide glue, and hand tools
www.toolsforworkingwood.com

LIE NIELSEN TOOLWORKS
Shooting plane, mortising chisels, and hand tools
www.lie-nielsen.com

PHILLY PLANES
My molding planes as well as other fine wooden handplanes
www.phillyplanes.co.uk

HOCK TOOLS
Handplane blades and hand tool kits
www.hocktools.com

OLD BROWN GLUE
The best liquid hide glue
www.oldbrownglue.com

METRIC EQUIVALENTS

INCHES	CENTIMETERS	MILLIMETERS	INCHES	CENTIMETERS	MILLIMETERS
1/8	0.3	3	13	33.0	330
1/4	0.6	6	14	35.6	356
3/8	1.0	10	15	38.1	381
1/2	1.3	13	16	40.6	406
5/8	1.6	16	17	43.2	432
3/4	1.9	19	18	45.7	457
7/8	2.2	22	19	48.3	483
1	2.5	25	20	50.8	508
1 1/4	3.2	32	21	53.3	533
1 1/2	3.8	38	22	55.9	559
1 3/4	4.4	44	23	58.4	584
2	5.1	51	24	61.0	610
2 1/2	6.4	64	25	63.5	635
3	7.6	76	26	66.0	660
3 1/2	8.9	89	27	68.6	686
4	10.2	102	28	71.1	711
4 1/2	11.4	114	29	73.7	737
5	12.7	127	30	76.2	762
6	15.2	152	31	78.7	787
7	17.8	178	32	81.3	813
8	20.3	203	33	83.8	838
9	22.9	229	34	86.4	864
10	25.4	254	35	88.9	889
11	27.9	279	36	91.4	914
12	30.5	305			

INDEX

If you like this book, you'll love *Fine Woodworking*.